Dedication

To the Givers of Gifts, my angel guides. This book is in thanksgiving to the Light Spirits that accompany me daily. They are very important and real in my life, thus deserve note and mention of their great wonders. Also to my seven grandchildren, Rebecca, Alexander, Nicholas, Matthew, Jacob, Brianne and Ryan who have been sent to me as my 'earthly angels'. Without God I am nothing; with God I am everything. I give thanks to God for all that I am, all that I do, and all I will ever do.

"Many of those who sleep in the dust of the earth shall awake. Some shall live forever, others shall be an everlasting horror and disgrace.

"But the wise shall shine brightly like the splendor the firmament, and those who lead the many to justice shall be like stars forever."
Daniel 12:2

Judy Hamilton

CONTENTS

v

Acknowledgements

I am indebted to the authors who shared their personal experiences in this volume. A special kind of courage is required to break through the front lines of speculation to create a new awareness.

An appreciative "thank you" to two people who went out of their way to help actualize this publication. My editor, Esther Supernault, is an author herself of five novels. She is intuitive and meticulous in her work. Randall Kabatoff is the book designer, project manager and owner of Vision Images in Edmonton, Alberta, Canada. He is a congenial, talented craftsman with many gifts.

I also thank the artists that submitted their creative works and all those that entered the competition. Last, but not least, I thank my husband Fred for the computer time, guidance and support during this project.

Judy Hamilton –
Winner of Angel Artwork Competition

Editor's Notes

I felt very honored to read these stories for the first time. There is an underlying sense of deep truth and awe, even celebration in every one of them. This, to me, is the greatest awareness of a Higher Power that guides, protects and loves us all. It is faith in its purest form. How tragic that people kept these stories secret for so many years, afraid of criticism and judgment from family and friends. Yet the mere simplicity and threads of similar incidents woven through these stories, from people who have never met, proves there is something more than their imaginations at work.

With only a few exceptions, these are stories written by the people who lived them - a first hand account of an actual experience. I have neither embellished nor changed any of the details of their stories. I edited only for punctuation and grammatical flow. What you will read is each event as it happened by those who witnessed it.

My wish to you is that after reading these stories, you will feel more comfortable sharing your own similar experiences - for we all have had them. Some of us, however, never recognized them for the miracles that they are!

Esther Supernault
Editor/writer

Michael Godet

Introduction

Today's society is eager for more information about heavenly beings and the world beyond. *HeartBeat Angels* will delight the curious with personal spiritual encounters - celestial adventures that are exciting, mysterious and scientifically unexplainable.

In order to add interest and variety to my book, I held a competition for the best story and the best angel artwork. The diverse stories came from all across North America, from people of all walks of life, from men, women and children. Each story is different and each offers insight into one's own life experience that we often call coincidence.

I wish to express a heartfelt "Thank You" to all who have shared their testimonials with such courage, openness and humility. I am privileged to have had this opportunity to be involved in such an important aspect of your life.

The purpose of *HeartBeat Angels* is to unveil the celestial secrets that many of us conceal. There is a purpose in each of us, and while many of us have been touched by God's hand, not everyone has made the decision to surrender. My interest is to reawaken our spirituality and listen to the seemingly insignificant messages we receive daily.

When I began this journey, little did I realize the diverse people I would meet. As strangers we connected on a spiritual 'common ground' and this led to a realization that we shared a common 'heartbeat'. This shared truth is evidence that amidst ordinary people, one finds something extraordinary and miraculous.

Understanding supernatural phenomena cannot be easily explained and is often difficult to accept. It is not certain why some individuals have supernatural experiences while others do not. From those that volunteered information about the encounters, the only common thread that I could find was that these people were of 'open mind' and perhaps somewhat 'child-like' in their hearts. Age, culture and life circumstances all differed. On occasion, spiritual intervention occurred at a turning point in their lives, such as illness or tragedy. Often this leads to the attraction of God's magnetism, the pulling force to know more, feel more, do more. I have found this to be so in my own case. I have that magnetism.

Most religions agree that angels exist and both the Old and New Testaments confirm that angels assist us. Yet many individuals are unable to open their minds and call these encounters merely coincidence or synchronicity at work. If we allow ourselves to become mirrors, then what we experience is a reflection of our 'true divine nature'-our higher selves.

The secret may be in letting go thus taking the first step to changing our limited mindset. Suddenly, we are on another path, we are listening for inner guidance. Children do not have difficulty accepting or explaining the appearance of angels. Many people question the mystical phenomena of fragrant odours, disappearances of objects, gentle touches and voices. However, those who experience this also claim an overwhelming feeling of peace and joy. A receptive attitude often leads to more experiences, however many have just one encounter.

Since the beginning of time, man dreamt of touching the sky and now spaceships give us this opportunity. Since the beginning of time, man connected with the spiritual world and, for a great many, this was lost. However, we can reconnect again. Amidst the darkness there is light and if we consider each minute as a special, precious gift, we find that life is an amazing dream, a miracle of heartbeats.

Amazingly, as I struggled to pull things together, events occurred that conspired to keep me from completion. There were many disappearing sentences, release forms lost in transit, computer confusion as stories began to appear under different titles or not at all. This lead to my own confusion and uncertainty but with guidance, I listened to my angels rather than my feelings. God also provided me with an abundance of energy, insight and friendship. *"For we are fellow workmen - joint promoters, laborers together - with and for God"* (Corinthians 3:9).

I invite you to immerse yourself in the wisdom that is so graciously shared. These essays assume the universality of life with evidence in favour of a life after death. It is my hope that *HeartBeat Angels* will help individuals become inspired and conscious of their experiences in everyday life. I invite you to send, fax, and E-mail those stories to be shared in the next *HeartBeat Angels* book to add to the amazing revelations that await printing.

Enjoy reading my friends, and with God's love our visionary paths will be experienced.

In the Spirit of Love,
Pauline Newman

Vance Hilton

CHAPTER 1

Angels Among Us

*"For He shall give His angels charge over you,
to keep you in all your ways."*
Psalm 91:11

Those who believe in a spiritual world step beyond the boundaries of the physical world. As humans we cannot see angels unless they reveal themselves to us. The visible world seems more real and sensible to us.

It is obvious that we do not have to do everything on our own because we have divine assistance. According to the Bible from Genesis to Revelation, God reveals his spiritual creatures to us through divine revelations and the world is brimming with spiritual beings.

The ancient world accepted and understood that angels were part of the created world. Today in our technological age we tend to forget God or keep him at a distance, as it is easy to dismiss God's plan of uniting the visible and the invisible.

Randall Kabatoff

Randall Kabatoff

The Trumpeting Angel

My name is Randall and I am a spiritually inspired photographer, artist and publisher. Over the last year I embraced the idea of creating images of the angelic realm of beings. So it was a pleasant affirmation when I came into contact with Pauline Newman who was looking for creative help to publish a book about angels. I agreed to design the book, share some of my images, and prepare the book for printing. I acknowledged the role of grace and I felt very grateful to be able to contribute to this project.

On March 9, 2001, mid way through the design of this book, I had a supper visit in a restaurant with Edward, a close friend. Among his many skills, talents and interests he is also blessed with "gifts of the spirit" or, as others may call him, a "psychic sensitive" with clairaudient and clairvoyant abilities (one dictionary defines a clairaudient as having the power of hearing or knowing about sounds beyond the range of hearing, while a clairvoyant has the power of knowing about things that are out of sight, also known as 'second sight').

During supper, I told Edward that I was working with Pauline to design *HeartBeat Angels*. I indicated that it was Pauline's desire to get these secret stories out into the public light where others can be encouraged and inspired by this information. I also indicated that it was bringing more awareness to me as well, and that I felt encouraged to allow these "winged ones" to play a more conscious part in my life. I said to Edward that Pauline was eager for the book to proceed to its publishing date "in God's good speed" because it would touch many lives.

As I spoke I could see he was very interested in what I was saying, but I noticed Edward's body twitch, as if some energy was running through him. I could see he was distracted by something. When I asked him what he was sensing he said an angel joined us! This is Edward's account of his experience:

> *The moment was felt before observed, a shock wave of energy that resonated through my endocrine system. When my eyes refocused it was there, above my companions right shoulder. I could not tell if it was male or female, even though it was naked. I don't think it matters, except perhaps to censors and such. I have seen many before, but this was a new type, more mature than an average cherub, but not a teen body either. It held a trumpet, as many seem to. From the trumpet hung a tapestry of symbols, glyphs designed to communicate to the subconscious. The tapestry was a rich burgandy-crimson, the letters in white silk embroidery.*
>
> *My companion inquired and I shared my vision. We laughed as we had just been discussing a project on angel stories. I realized that my body had first reacted when I had thought to contribute, and as that thought occurred I became aware of a warm feeling spreading from my left ear through my body as the angel sounded its trumpet softly for me to hear. Thank you divine guidance.*

I thought this trumpet holding angel was heralding an affirmative message of grace that this book must be made and shared with others. If I needed a spiritual sign I got it!

I later learned that this musical instrument is called a "Herald Trumpet". The dictionary defines a herald as one who carries messages, makes announcements; a messenger. Referring to a concordance I discovered that the trumpet is mentioned over one hundred times in the Bible and it is often used as a metaphor for God's voice.

4

This spiritual symbol kept coming to my awareness and as I worked on the design of the book I came across many illustrations of angels holding herald trumpets. I grew more intrigued with the meaning of this spiritual symbol.

I started calling music stores and organizations around Edmonton to see who had a herald trumpet that I could borrow to photograph for the book. But the herald trumpet is a rare instrument. On March 30, just days before the book was to go to the printer, I made many calls in a last effort to find this special trumpet. I had some leads but no success that day.

That afternoon I went to Jacquie's house, my wife's mother, to locate a photograph of some angelic looking clouds my wife Sherry had taken. Sherry told me to look in a corner bookshelf in her old bedroom. When I knelt down to this corner shelf I saw a box with a picture of a ceramic cherub holding a herald trumpet! Yet another appearance. The ornament belonged to Jacquie and I thought of all the places in her big house to store it, it was placed here for me to find. I opened the box and found the cherub decoration. But it was missing its herald trumpet and this is why it was not on display. Another sign and it delighted me.

It was hours later that I saw the humor and irony in this. I was missing a real herald trumpet to photograph, and even this angel, correspondingly, was missing his. We were both empty handed. Now I am intrigued with the deeper meaning of the herald trumpet and I know that I shall find my "voice" and publish more images and stories about this theme.

Randall Kabatoff and Edward Dumaine

Angel Farm

Nature has been generous to me. So much spirituality surrounds my one hundred and sixty-acre home near Lake Wabamun, Alberta, Canada. On this day, friends and strangers from Asia came with Canadian and local escorts to feel and 'touch' the spirituality people find on my land. They did not speak, only looked and searched, having long waited for this day, this moment. Eyes and ears did their work of enabling the spiritual to fly, to float and to touch. Dozens of eyes grew larger. A gasp, surprise and joy engulfed each person's mind and heart. They had found an angel and they knew it. Only the air told us we were not alone. Each one sought more solitude; each one found her own angel and knew it to be true, not imagination. Every second was cherished, as the breeze from each one's angel hovered over and around each one's own spiritual world of angels. Faces smiled with joy, eyes shed tears quietly. We realized that an angel touched each one as they walked the trail through the evergreens that day.

Every one of the women became a new person inside and out. In silence, we returned to the home to a living room full of inspiration. A large frame with the writings, in Arabic, of the entire Quran held the women of various faiths entranced. Those who knew the Arabic language were fascinated, wanting to read it, wanting to know the meanings of the beautiful letters, words and sentences. We talked and enjoyed our special tea from South Africa, a gift from my new friends in Capetown.

Slowly, one by one, each woman reflected on her walk. They all felt "an unbelievably beautiful touch of an angel". Many angels surrounded one of the women. She could not move but she felt a feather light touch, as each angel passed closely to her hair and her cheek. Everyone had a special experience. It is not easy to speak of such an experience. You only want to savour this joy within your body, recording it in your mind, hopefully to share with others, especially children.

On my return to Edmonton later that day, I drove eastward towards 142 Street. Suddenly, a car appeared, coming directly at me. The driver must not have seen me or had lost control of the car. In a flash, my car was 'lifted' over this car and I found myself driving north towards Stony Plain Road!

My own experiences began at the age of four. My father was a Sufi Sheik, who had the power to heal and to put out country fires with a prayer as he stood on a hay-stack, on a farm near our home. All of our family, even my formerly Methodist mother, had angel experiences.

Now, at seventy-six years, my belief in angels has never changed. As a Muslim child, I prayed to the angel on my right shoulder and to the angel on my left shoulder, day and night. It is not easy to share this with my readers but as a Sufi, I received a gift in Tetwan, Morocco, many years ago. I have a great responsibility, as a Sufi, to others who walk on my path. My angels are always with me.

Bless all of you who read of this experience.

Dr. Lila Fahlman

Anne Dixon's Story

Anne Dixon lived alone in our small town of Stony Plain, Alberta, Canada. Her home was a unique vintage apartment built in the 1920's. We became friends when she visited my retail store to buy her wool for knitting. She loved making baby outfits for her friend's children and grandchildren. Later, she made them for mine as well.

I knew Anne was not feeling well for some years but she refused to see a doctor. She once confided in me that she probably had cancer, yet whenever I offered to take her to a doctor or the hospital, she would say, "What for?" That was the way she wanted it to be. I kept insisting but she kept refusing.

Anne was a widow whose only child had died years ago. She had told me that she had a brother and sister living in Edmonton so I asked for their names or phone numbers in case of an emergency. She refused, saying that she had had a disagreement with them and was not speaking to them.

Through the years, I often brought her samples of Ukrainian food from one of my grandchildren's christenings or birthdays. She enjoyed this but always said, "What did you do this for? I have lots of food."

One day the hospital called and said that Anne was in the hospital and asking for me. When I arrived, I realized how ill she was. I got goose bumps when she told me her amazing story.

She said that she had fallen in her apartment and hit her head, laying on the floor for several days before I came to her rescue. Yet this was the first time I had seen her in almost a month! She insisted that a lady came to her apartment and gave her some tuna and fruit to eat. With this strength, she was able to crawl to the telephone and call 911.

Anne had two doors to her ancient apartment. One was a steel door at the bottom entrance. The second door was at the top of the stairs opening into her apartment. Both were kept locked at all times. I asked Anne who had unlocked the doors, since she was lying on the floor in pain and could not move. At first she told me that I had unlocked the doors for the ambulance men. Then she remembered that I wasn't there.

"Anne," I said, "this was your angel helping you!"

"I guess so," she replied.

Her doctor explained to me that Anne was probably on the floor for three days. She could not have moved, let alone sat up or crawl anywhere. In fact, she had a broken back!

Anne asked me to check her apartment and pay several bills. When I entered her home, it definitely needed cleaning! On the kitchen counter lay a half tin of spoiled tuna, an old-fashioned can opener, and some fruit. I was so delighted at this find that I hurriedly cleaned her apartment, then immediately went to my shop and made her a green 12" abaca angel. Eventually, I persuaded Anne to give me her brother's phone number. He and his sister came immediately.

Anne was transferred to a city hospital for cancer surgery. I told her to keep the green angel by her bed and think of me if she was lonely. She died in the hospital after her surgery. Although her body was cremated, I could feel her presence over my right shoulder at the memorial service. Her sister wanted to return the angel but I convinced her to keep it as a reminder that her sister Anne was safe in her new home.

Pauline Newman

Loved Beyond Measure

I have had so many experiences it is hard to know which one I should write about. However, I have to tell you how it all started.

My spiritual capabilities began when I was a little girl about five years of age. I ran into an old, oak table leg and came out 'second best' from it. I looked down and saw blood soaking into my white dress. I had cracked my skull from the top down to just above my right eye, leaving me in mental shock.

I remember seeing bright lights, shimmering faces and strange people wearing gold gowns. How odd they looked. My body felt icy cold, then hot and I appeared to be floating. Then I heard soft, whispered words telling me that I had to return. Immeasurable love kept embracing me, giving this experience an unforgettable impact on my mind and soul. I felt I was with angels.

Later, my mom revealed to me that nobody had expected me to ever talk or walk again due to my memory loss. She never wished to enlighten me with many other details. I did, however, recover to some extent. One day, I was standing in the middle of our newly cleared field staring up at an incredible illumination cascading down on my head. A hand lightly touched me, caressing my chin, while a voice told me that I was of the "wind love" and to "go with the wind." Flashing stars caught and held my attention; all I could think of was - 'Grandmother'.

Out of fear, I ignored my gift and spent many years trying to be like everyone else. Suddenly, I was struck with terminal cancer. Using my gift, which I had received as a little girl, I eliminated the cancer. After that, I went on to experience different cultures and to live in many parts of

North America. I had the opportunity to meet many people working on their spiritual paths. I met tarot readers, mediums, physics and faith healers. Then I met the Wiccan Wise Women, Aboriginal medicine people. I worked with many of these people and acquired many experiences. My life has been full of angelic and spiritual wonderment.

Another amazing experience happened on a snowy country road while I was driving home one night. Suddenly a flashing, bright light filled my vision. I slammed on my brakes and saw a shimmering face with hands held up to stop me. It was Saint Michael. My startled eyes saw an angel change into a deer and bound off into the dark, forested wilderness. The Archangel Michael saved a woodland creature from a cruel and unjust death and saved my truck from being damaged.

I have been one of the fortunate ones with intuitive power. I have passed through many test cycles involving interference from other sources. The Divine Powers are forever guiding and teaching me. Without a doubt, I am loved beyond measure.

B. J. Marcou

Randall Kabatoff

A Band of Angels

May of 1997 was an extremely difficult time for me. My husband had died unexpectedly at the age of forty-six and I was thrown into post-traumatic depression. I found it very difficult to leave the house. One day, a good friend of mine insisted I come over for a light lunch. Since she knew I had a doctor's appointment in the afternoon, I could not use the excuse again that I did not leave the house. The luncheon went well but I was left with not enough time to go home for a rest. Still, it was too early for my appointment.

Then something quite out of the ordinary happened. It was a Wednesday and I spotted a garage sale sign along the road. I thought how strange to have such a sale mid week. Being an avid garage sale person, I wondered how I could have missed the sign when I drove to my friend's. With some time to waste, I stopped. Stranger still, there was no garage and no line up of cars. The sign pointed to the house so I cautiously knocked on the door.

I was told that an estate sale was in progress and that most of the larger items were taken. Still, I was welcome to look around. I found some beautiful needlework and a quilt. When I asked the person present for the price, I was told the granddaughter would be right with me to answer any questions. The granddaughter was about my age and we began a conversation on her granny's collection of crafts and how a lot of the knowledge was not passed along to the next generation. She then told me what a hard time she had when her granny passed away in May. Only the faith that her granny had taught her sustained her. I never mentioned that my husband had passed away about the same time.

Then this strange look came over the granddaughter's face and she seemed to be staring at something behind me. Suddenly, with a presence that made - and to this day still makes - the hair on my arms stand up, this lady stated that I must have just suffered the loss of a close loved one. I asked her why she thought that. She replied, "I see a whole band of angels around you and they are there to protect you and guide you during this troubling time."

I never saw this lady again nor do I remember where the house was. But I no longer believe that things happen solely by coincidence. At that particular time, I was in desperate need of an affirmation. This event will stay with me forever.

Psalm 91:11: "For He shall give His angels charge over you, to keep you in all your ways".

Katherine

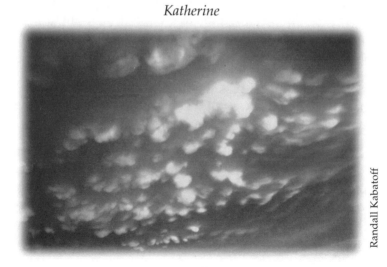

Randall Kabatoff

My Little Angel

Many times in my life, I have been lucky to have a special ethereal angel come to me with messages. She is in the form of a four-year-old girl. To my amazement, I have mentioned her appearance to others and they can describe what she looks like and how she appears to them as well. She is a very busy little girl.

She came to me in 1998, at a time when I struggled with many things in my life. One night she appeared at the end of my bed, standing in a glow of light. The second night she came again, giving me a strong push on the right side of my body. It was as if she were saying, "Wake Up! Wake Up!"

At the time, I was looking after my brother's German Shepherd while he and his wife were away on holidays. That first night, I closed the dog off in the basement with a piece of plywood but by morning, the dog was in my bedroom. The second night, the dog lay on a sleeping bag beside my bedroom door. When I felt the push, I groggily thought it was the dog waking me because she needed to go outside. But when I turned on the light, the dog was still asleep, undisturbed.

The next morning, I phoned a friend from whom I had taken a spiritual course and described the two nights' phenomenon. She replied, "Grace, she was not waking you out your sleep; she is telling you to wake up in your life."

In less than three days my life took a turn for the better, though I am still not clear as to what awaits me in the future.

Around this same time, a friend arrived from British Columbia, Canada, to spend Christmas with her folks. We happened to connect one day and I started telling her about this little girl. My friend not only described this little angel, she told me how this little girl had saved her parent's home. The little girl had alerted the parents to a bulb, which had never worked, on an overhead light. Apparently, it was not the bulb but the wiring in the fixture itself that would have eventually shorted out and possibly caused a fire.

So here is more proof of this beautiful angel doing her work all around us. What a sweet being she is!

Grace Oranchuk

Father Douglas

Angel of Sunshine

Right after my brother's tragic death, I tried desperately to get a sense that his spirit was at peace. The thought of his spirit being in turmoil left me paralyzed with an overwhelming sadness. My life was like a turbulent storm. At night I would lay awake for hours in anguish. In the mornings I felt exhausted and unable to face the day. I tried so hard to be strong. I wanted to gain a sense that my brother was all right, so I prayed to God to show me a sign, any sign. I had no expectations of what the sign would be. I just wanted some connection so that I could begin to heal and gain strength.

One week after my brother died, I stopped at a friend's house to visit. As I drove away, I looked back in case my friend was watching me from the window. When I left the house, the street was quiet and no one was around. Yet when I looked back, a little girl stood on the sidewalk, looking and smiling right at me. She certainly had not been there before. I would have seen her walking down the street. I was so astonished; I asked her where she had come from. It was like she came from out of nowhere!

A strong feeling of joy flooded my body. I knew right away why she had come to visit me. I felt tears come to my eyes, tears of complete happiness and hope. She was only about three years old, so I said to her. "Be careful. Don't get run over."

With that, she giggled the most beautiful, joyous giggle and waved, then she ran off down the sidewalk. I will never forget the way she looked at me. She conveyed to me a message of calm with her eyes alone.

From this angelic visit, I gained a strong sense that my brother was at peace. Now I was able to close my eyes at night and focus on the warmth and love that comes from the Divine. My prayers were answered and I was able to sleep and gain strength. I was able to go back to my job of working with troubled youth.

God helped me gain strength so that I could continue helping others. Naturally the path to peace has been a struggle after the devastating death of my brother, but I do believe God sent me a messenger to let me know that my brother is no longer in pain. God bless my angel for giving me a ray of sunshine during a terrible storm.

Yvonne Law

Randall Kabatoff

Angel of Acknowledgement

Seven years ago I felt stress from several situations; a recent move, a change in life style, closing a business. I was also a lonely bachelor and I wanted to find a life partner. Consequently, I was questioning where my life was going and I wanted insight.

Through a friend, I heard about a woman, Judy, who was said to be a good astrology reader. I called her and Judy said she did readings occasionally and financial remuneration was not necessary for me to receive a reading.

On the evening of the appointment we sat at a table in the dining area of a spacious house near Edmonton, Alberta, Canada. Judy, a pleasant woman in her mid thirties, was of Aboriginal descent. I soon learned that Judy was a very sensitive person, with psychic gifts or "gifts of the spirit". I felt she was trustworthy and sincere.

As the reading progressed, I grew more focused on the message shared with me. While there were several points I was pleased to hear about myself, there were, however, messages that were painful because it meant I must change if I was to grow as a person and progress in my life. Rather than shut down at the points that made me feel uncomfortable, I decided to stay receptive and open to what was being freely shared with me.

The more I focused on this session the deeper Judy went into reading my chart. She appeared to be relaying a lot of inspired or intuited messages. I was listening intently to one insightful message after another. She clarified with examples so that I would better grasp the information.

After concentrating together for almost an hour, the meeting was quite charged with energy. Judy, who was totally focused, had a lot of emotion in her voice. All of a sudden she bolted upright, shrieked, and reverently bowed her head and shielded her eyes with both her hands. It was as if some light was blinding her. She was clearly very agitated and upset. As she gasped for breath, I asked her what the matter was, and she reluctantly peaked towards me and stole a glance about fifteen feet behind me.

"There is an angel in the room!" She moaned. "I don't like it when something like this happens".

This was totally unexpected for both of us. I looked behind me. I saw a wall, a window and a kitchen, but no angel. Judy, however could obviously see, with what some call the gift of "second sight", the clear presence of another being.

It took her several minutes to calm down and to lower her hands completely from her eyes. In contrast I was interested and, in an innocent sort of way, receptive to the angel that joined us.

Once Judy had calmed down somewhat, in a mood of reverence and respect, she described the angel to me. The angel had a female form, with blond flowing hair, wearing a white glowing, translucent gown. She was hovering in the air, lying horizontally on her right side, floating about six feet above the floor.

In contrast to Judy I was cautiously desiring to connect with this spiritual being. I was not at all sure what the protocol was for angelic meetings. After a brief consideration of the situation I asked if I could communicate with the angel. Judy sighed and reluctantly agreed to assist in my request.

I wanted to know why the angel arrived. I was told the angel is here to acknowledge my "breakthrough". It was better now, at forty years of age, for me to 'wake up', 'to get it' then when I am seventy, as I still had 'earth time' to learn and grow and change.

Encouraged by the answers and the willingness of the angel to communicate, I asked the angel several questions and Judy continued to relay to me what she heard the angel answer. This is part of what we talked about.

I told the angel I was a photographer interested in publishing a book from the point of view of nature, of 'Mother Earth'. I said that I wanted to interview Mother Earth and ask her what images of Earth she would like people to see and what Mother Earth would like to say to people today. The angel replied that Earth is a living being like us, who feels and has emotions just like people do. The Earth is in pain because of the damage done to her body by humans. The angel encouraged me to go out into nature, as I did as a young boy, and watch the clouds and connect with nature for messages. I was told I had forgotten that I did this as a child.

I felt the spirit world had acknowledged my willingness to take some hard looks at the areas that I needed to change. I felt some comfort that I was not alone in my struggles, and that my life progress was being observed, supported and encouraged.

After a time Judy proceeded with the reading and the lessons continued. I felt joy as the meeting progressed. Later she said that she now could hear the voices of a number of angels who had also apparently arrived, but she could not see them. She said it sounded like they were celebrating. A celestial party was on! It was a celebration that another person had 'woken up' to some facts about his life and how he could grow as a human being.

Randall Kabatoff

Near Death

In 1975, I had an experience that saved my life and created a spiritual contact which still exists today. At that time, I lived in Oshawa, Ontario, Canada. I suffered from severe allergies, particularly in late summer with all the pollen and ragweed in full bloom. As I grew older my asthma became harder to control, especially the ragweed reaction. Drugs barely helped. It became a trial and error game for me and for my doctors to find something which worked.

I knew that weather controlled my condition but this was the 70's with little research done on pollution, chemicals and drugs. My system weakened further and by late August I was in deep trouble, surviving on cortisone, prednisone and other dangerous drugs. I gasped for air and stayed indoors most of the time. Finally I ended up in the hospital, taking dangerous drugs intravenously. I remember the doctor's warning the nurses that I was not to fall asleep or be left alone. The medication helped me relax and I soon fell asleep. I remember going into a long tunnel.

Days later, I awoke in a confused state, unable to focus. Noise agitated me and I couldn't remember things. They moved me to a private room but I couldn't get out of bed by myself and I couldn't remember if I had washed or changed my clothes that day. When the nurses helped me to the sink, I would fall down. I asked God to help me remember and to bring me home to my three children.

To keep track of my visitors, I had them write down their names and the time they were in so I could tell my husband when he came. I recall my sister and her daughter coming to help me. They both had to hold me as they washed my hair. Their voices seemed to be so far away as they fussed about my appearance. I had to write down my phone number so I could phone my children daily. I asked my husband to bring in a painting of our three children which I had received for Mother's Day. He hung it so I could see them whenever I was awake.

By now my arms were black and blue from all the needles. Sometimes my visitors left in tears. In my confused state, I wondered why they were so sad.

I was in the hospital about six weeks when, early one morning, I started to choke. When I came to, I saw a lady dressed in white standing at the foot of my bed. She appeared to be two or three feet off the floor, looking transparent against the wall. I can still recall her soft voice telling me not to take any more medicine. She went on to say that I would be home in three days if I listened to her. I was sure I would forget the instructions as I drifted off to sleep.

At 6:00 a.m., the nurse came in with my medications. I refused to take them, told her of my vision, and demanded to see my doctor. Unfortunately, it was Dr. Smith's day off. At lunchtime, it was medication time again. And again I refused, getting myself into trouble with the nurses.

To my amazement, by the afternoon I was strong enough to pick up the phone book and look for my doctor's number. With two pages of Smiths, I'm not sure how I picked the right Dr. Smith, but I did. When he came to see me, I told him about the lady in white and where she stood. He sat for a long time then asked me to read from a book. I could neither focus my eyes nor count backwards from ten. Suddenly, some messages for Dr. Smith came into my head. I wasn't sure where they came from but I passed them on to him. The next day, he sent me to a psychiatrist. I had messages for him too! Unfortunately, no one believed my story.

I insisted that I was going home to my family in three days and I refused to take any more pills. I heard all the arguments about decreasing the medication gradually but I stood my ground. By the third day, I had enough strength to dress, pack my belongings and walk without falling down. And I went home.

Yet whenever I talked about the lady in white to friends, they wouldn't believe me. They said that I was 'spun out' on the medication, that I just imagined the vision. Soon I stopped talking about the wonderful visitor who saved my life.

Only recently have I started sharing my experience once again. The secret kept hidden for so many years is now shared with you. My spiritual growth became easier and faster once I learned to trust my intuition, my inner guidance, my angels and the authentic power that I have. Since this first experience, I have had many more visions and messages. I am thankful that I believe in myself, in my angels, and in God.

Pauline Newman

Randall Kabatoff

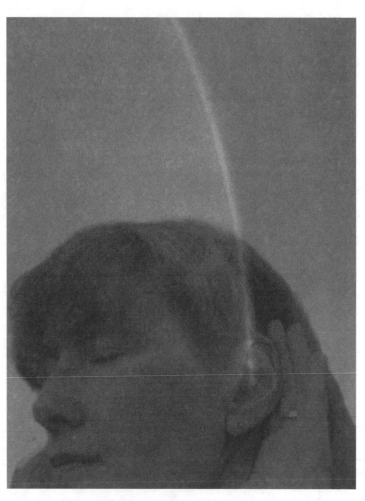

Randall Kabatoff

CHAPTER 2

Voices of Angels

*"My sheep hear my voice, and I know them
And they follow me."*
John 10:27

The better we understand how angels work and minister to our needs, the better we appreciate God's loving hand and guidance. Furthermore, the belief that angels guide natural events helps us to question certain assumed laws of nature. There is a popular notion that we live in a mechanical world where God's presence is not needed because we can create all things by our intelligence. Yet the whispers in our ear cannot be assumed to be our own idea. Those that listen to the voices with an open heart and mind learn extraordinarily that spiritual beings help lead us back to God's original plan. The new millennium calls us to reunite with the heavenly beings that God created.

Larissa Dunning

Voices

have never seen my guardian angel but I have heard him at four very crucial points in my life. Twenty-five years ago, I was deeply depressed. We had just moved to Ottawa and I was alone and lonely with a small son and very colicky baby daughter. One day, my husband offered to watch the children while I went for a walk and some fresh air. I wandered into an abandoned yard and sat on a snow-covered water fountain. I wondered about life, its purpose and why I had to live it. Then a voice said, "No, Esther, you have lots to do yet." I spun around to see who had spoken but I was totally alone. It was a male voice, neither young nor old, with a hint of gentle laughter in it. It cheered me and I returned home, calmer and more peaceful than I had felt in months.

Eight years later, I stopped along a narrow country road to throw away some fish heads and bones I didn't want our Irish Setter finding. As I flung them, my wedding ring flew off my finger and out into the night. I was horrified. The road had at least eight inches of snow and the ditches were drifted full. I stood in the headlights of my truck and cried. My husband had given me this beautifully crafted ring when I graduated from nursing four years earlier.

The same voice that I had heard in Ottawa said, "Walk ten steps ahead and three to your right."

I didn't question it, didn't even think. I just walked it. Looking down, I couldn't see anything. Whimpering and weeping, I turned around. There, just two inches from the toe of my boot, sparkling in the headlights, was my ring! I vaguely remember driving the fifteen miles to my University class, too dazed to dim my lights for oncoming traffic.

I lost my ring again a few years later while playing volleyball. We were playing in a small clearing surrounded by heavy bush. Again, the voice told me, "It's by the boards." Sure enough, at the back of the clearing was a pile of gray, weathered boards. My ring was sitting in the middle of the very top board. Who was I to argue word meanings!

Five years ago, my daughter was very ill, in and out of the hospital for months. They say a mother's prayers are the most powerful in the universe. When she prays for her child, the angels come running. So I prayed, as did many of our friends and family. One night, as I drifted off to sleep, the voice said, "You have been praying so hard, for so long, it is time your prayers were answered." And they were - within the month. Today, my daughter is healthy and happy once again.

These incidents, and many others, have given me an unshakable belief in God. He is always there to guide us, protect us and help us. All we have to do is ask, listen, and give thanks.

Thank you Lord, for your most precious messengers!

Esther Supernault

Conversation in the Night

I have been on speaking terms with my angels for as long as I can remember. Even when I was a child they whispered in my ear, keeping me from danger and pushing me back if I got too daring. It wasn't until I had been married for several years that they and I were put to the test.

After five years of trying to conceive and another year waiting to adopt, we finally got the call to pick up a six-week old baby girl. She was beautiful with dark hair and dark brown eyes. We called her Natalie. She was the first grandchild for our parents, so everyone doted on her.

I couldn't bear to be away from her. Where I went, she went. Even at night, her bassinet lay at my side. Her daddy would sit and talk to her, planning and promising to always be there for her.

The days went pleasantly by. We waited for the three months to pass before we could go before a judge for the final adoption signing. One evening, the week before we were to go to court, my husband answered the phone. When he turned around after a short conversation, he was crying. "She's changed her mind; she wants her back."

We were all devastated and our parents were angry that the mother had left it so late before informing us. There was a lot of crying that night and the following week. We were so confused. One night, I could not sleep and wondered how I could get through this turmoil. My angels started talking to me, making me see reason as to why this child was not meant to be with me. I finally understood that my child was out there somewhere; we just had to find each other. Once I realized that, I found peace and calmed down.

A month later we met that special child at the agency. When I pulled back the blanket, I laughed out loud. She looked like a chubby sparrow. Her fair hair had a big curl combed up on the top of her head and she smiled at the sound of my voice. I think that she knew she belonged to us. We called her Katy. A few years later, we adopted our son and our family was complete.

Katy is now grown and married with children of her own and I can't imagine my life without her in it.

We told our children in their teens that if they wanted to find their birth mothers, we would help them. Not an easy task, since we immigrated to Canada from England when the children were very young. When Katy had her children, she decided to search for her birth mother. My husband and I helped her. In fact, I was the first person to talk to the woman on the telephone. I thanked her for bringing Katy into the world for us to love and cherish. She is such a treasure. I feel no fear of losing Katy to her birth mother because my angels told me thirty years ago what was meant to be.

Jacqueline Owens

Jacqueline Cunningham

The Nightlight

One year ago, my room-mate Paul and his daughter, Makeda, moved out of my house. We had been together for five years. After they left, I was alone in a large house. I decided to buy a nightlight. This really didn't help me because I still felt afraid to go to sleep at night. Consequently, I was awake until the wee hours most nights.

Then, one night, a voice and presence came to me saying, "Buy an angel light that looks like me."

Ironically, the next day, I found an angel-shaped night-light at a garage sale and quickly snapped it up. Since that time, I have never felt afraid and now sleep the whole night through with ease and harmony. I feel that the Angel is taking care and watching over me. What a comforting feeling!

Deloris Jack

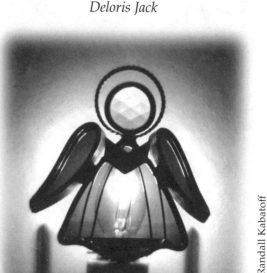

Randall Kabatoff

Judy Hamilton

Who Called My Name?

On a cool fall day, I drove home from Edmonton to Stony Plain, Alberta, Canada, about thirty-seven kilometers away. There was no snow but a lot of fog since Stony Plain is about five miles north of the North Saskatchewan River. I approached an area where the fog is usually very thick. With trees on the north and south side of the road, a lot of deer and moose crossed there. It was about 1:00 o'clock in the morning with no traffic as I hurried along.

Out of nowhere someone called my name. I wrote it off to being too tired and half asleep. Again it called, much louder and sharper. It was so clear that I quickly shifted down to a lower gear, not touching my brakes. When I entered the foggy area, I was moving at a crawl.

Just ahead were tracks from tires skidding across the highway. Obviously, vehicles had gone into the ditch on both sides earlier in the evening. They were all gone now. I thanked God and my Guardian Angels and proceeded home very carefully.

Grace Oranchuk

Randall kabatoff

Angels to Protect and Love

For as long as I can remember, I've always believed in angels. My parents raised me to believe that angels always looked over me and gave me guidance when lost. I never understood what that meant - until I really became lost.

Like many people, I went through a time in my life when I just didn't want to go on anymore. I saw no point in sticking around; there wasn't anything here for me. As I fell further and further into depression, I started thinking about death. What was it really? Did I want to go down that path? I pictured what it would be like if I just disappeared out of people's lives. I always saw myself in a hospital bed. I even knew why I was in the hospital - a car hit me. Now, this image didn't come to me in a dream. It came to me whenever I was in a car or crossing a street or lying down. It always came out of nowhere, yet I knew I would be fine. I also knew that people would show me, for that brief little moment in time, how much I truly meant to them. I never actually thought about this image. I just figured it was something that I wanted, not that it would happen.

When that day came, it was one of the happiest I had felt in awhile. The idea of a car hitting me was the last thing on my mind. As I look back now, I remember something telling me not to cross the street that day. Something also told me to go to my friend's dad and ask him to give me a ride, or to miss the bus and catch the next one. I never listened. When I saw the bus, I just ran towards it. I did look both ways as I crossed the street, but not very well. I remember that I had a strong feeling not to finish crossing that road, the same feeling I had been having all day. It became stronger and stronger, yet I still ignored it.

The amazing thing is that I shouldn't be here today. I ended up being thrown forty-five feet into the air and landing on my back. The only thing that prevented my spine and neck from being broken is the way I landed on my backpack. It saved my life, really. I walked out of that accident with only a few bruises and scars. I truly had something or someone looking over me that day.

My angels gave me warnings and when I ignored them, they still protected me and saved me. Also, they gave me a slap on the head to smarten me up and make me realize that there are tons of people in the world that care and love me.

You just have to open your eyes sometimes.

Amanda Shrieves

Maureen Stefaniuk

Messages Come In Many Forms

I have learned that angels give messages in many forms, not just the way that we expect or are looking for. I have been working with my angels for a long time now and have come to take quite a lot for granted. But I remember the freshness and the vitality of those first experiences, which lead me to trust and honor my communications with my 'teammates'.

I have known that I had angels for quite awhile and was very excited when I learned how to communicate with them. This ability was not only comforting but also useful! At that time, I worked two jobs. Coming home from my evening job, I had a choice of two buses, which stopped on different streets. Unfortunately, if I happened to stand at the wrong bus stop, I didn't have time to get to the right one before the bus rolled away. Since the bus stops are in a dimly lit area near the downtown section of a large city, I did not want to wait around. Every night I would ask my angels which stop to stand at, and every time they answered by giving me goose bumps on a certain part of my arm. One night, I missed the first bus and was a little upset until I got on the second bus and found an old friend sitting there (just waiting for me - if he'd only known it!).

But messages don't always come that way. Sometimes we need to listen with our ears, our eyes, mouths or any other sensory organ — including our brain, which is very sensitive and often gives us hunches.

I had a roommate whom I liked very much. She was like a sister to me and I valued our friendship. One Thursday night, as they were leaving for a trip, her boyfriend picked a fight with me. I'm not proud to say that I fell into the trap and we had a rousing argument. When they left, he and I were still furious. Of course, when I had calmed down, I felt very badly and wished that I could somehow make things right but I had no way of contacting them. I really did not want to lose the friendship and worried that the quarrel had damaged it. I was miserable the next day, just getting through it the best I could, with no energy or enthusiasm at all. At lunchtime, instead of walking outside as I usually did, I found myself meandering through a mall, gazing listlessly at nothing in particular. Then the mall music broke through my fog - A Beach Boys' song with the chorus: "Don't worry baby, everything will be all right . . . ." For the first time that day, I smiled. Then I practically ran back to work so I could have a couple of quiet minutes to check things out with my angels. "Yes," came the answer, "Everything is all right, there is no need to worry."

I didn't stop worrying altogether but I did allow most of the pressure to lift. I spent a very pleasant weekend. When my roommate returned, she said, "Oh, by the way, he felt very badly for the way he acted. He wanted to call you Friday night to apologize but I told him it would be all right, that you wouldn't worry about it." Then I knew a sure thing - the music was a message and I got it!

Since those times, I have had many experiences which have taught me the value of listening with all my senses. I have learned both from the times I listened and from the times I did not. The most wonderful thing in all these years is that I am finally understanding deep in my heart, not just in my head, that I am not going through this life alone. I have friends, I have help and I have love. I have everything I need to be abundantly, successfully and marvelously happy. Thank you angels!

Janet Hill

Randall Kabatoff

CHAPTER 3

Loved Ones
Who Return

*"After this Jesus revealed himself
again to his Disciples"*
John 21:1

Spiritual encounters seem to come into our awareness in whatever form that we allow. Stories of angels in the Bible tell us of their existence and presence in many different aspects. Hebrew 1: 14 writes about the angels mission to assist us toward salvation, "ministering spirits sent forth to serve, for the sake of those who are to obtain salvation." The modern mind tends to be sceptical with what it cannot prove with evidence, and accepts only what it can physically see and believe to be visible.

Randall Kabatoff

My Angel, My Grandma

My Grandma, Bernice Ethel Boehlke, was going to live forever. At least, that is what I thought until November 16, 1991. She was seventy years old, enjoying her long deserved retirement. Grandpa was twenty-five years older than Grandma and had died at the age of eighty, twelve years earlier. Grandma never remarried. She had a loving family and many friends to keep her busy.

My family is from Athabasca, Alberta, Canada, which is a two-hour drive north of Edmonton. After completing high school, I moved to Edmonton where I worked for the provincial government. I missed home and lived for the weekends when I could return to my family, especially Grandma. She and I had a special, very close relationship.

On Saturday, November 16, 1991, about six o'clock in the evening, Grandma was driving home from Athabasca. She lived about twenty minutes north of town. Her car came over a hill and mysteriously appeared on the wrong side of the road. She headed straight into a crew cab, a four by four truck, which totally crushed the top of her car. She was killed instantly.

That weekend, I had decided not to go home and was in Edmonton when I heard the news. Devastated and bewildered, I cried and cried until totally exhausted. I was so upset because I didn't have a chance to say goodbye.

As I lay in bed waiting to fall asleep, Grandma came to me. I couldn't believe that she was there with me, comforting me. I felt so peaceful as she hugged me and said, "It's okay!" I felt so excited. She had come to say good-bye.

Ten years have passed, yet not one day goes by that I don't think of her. Her return and comforting love helped me to grieve her death in a more healthy, positive way.

She does live on spiritually because she still helps when I ask her. Four years ago, I was trying to quit smoking. I asked Grandma to help me stop the craving. I remember asking her then putting down my cigarettes and never looking at another package of them again. I know it was her strength that helped me quit.

She is my Angel and always will be.

Tracee Biletski

Randall Kabatoff

Stephen's Visit

From earliest memory, my childhood was wracked with horrific nightmares. Night after night, I dreaded the trek upstairs to my bed. I fell asleep to the echoing sounds of Gregorian chants in my head, overwhelmed by an anguished sense of doom. Frequently in these dreams, I fell to my death, waking only after I had broken my dream body on large gray rocks jutting away from the base of a tall and cheerless castle.

In these nightmares, I was a stranger to myself, wearing a different body and living a life far apart from that of my childhood. Yet I would awake from these dreams with my screams still echoing in the dark. My mother often came upstairs to comfort me and encourage me to return to sleep. Just as many times, however, I awoke to a silent household, my siblings and parents still sleeping peacefully. Being awake was almost as terrifying as sleeping. I prayed for someone to wake up, to reassure me and allow me to exchange my panic for the oblivion of a dreamless sleep.

One night, a few months after my eleventh birthday, I had the castle dream again. In this dream, I was a slender boy of about twelve, with black hair in a pageboy cut. I wore a bloomer type of outfit that ballooned over my hips and thighs, with wrinkled tights and oversized slippers. I had a message to deliver. I was on one of the highest levels of the castle, making my way down a damp and drafty hallway. My passing caused the bad-smelling torches to waver and throw out black smoke as they burned in their holders on the walls above my head.

As I approached the door I was seeking, I heard loud voices inside from two angry men. They sat at right angles to one another at a long table. One had his back to the door where I stood. Bowls of watery-looking oatmeal sat before them. I knew that none of us spoke English. The large, dark-haired man with his back to me suddenly reached out his huge meaty hand, grabbed his companion and snapped the man's neck with an audible crack. The dead man fell face down into his bowl, splashing its contents. His murderer sat gloating, a wide grin splitting his dark face to reveal uneven and dirty-looking teeth.

I must have inadvertently made a sound. Turning and seeing me there, he beckoned me closer. I remained frozen in the doorway. The man stood and menacingly moved towards me. Instantly, I shuddered and raced back down the hallway, in an incoherent panic. Blindly, I ran past the stairwell and arrived helplessly at the end of the hallway. I was by an open window overlooking a barren view of upturned rocks far below. Outside, a pale moon cast light and shadow equally. I heard the murderer coming closer, his steps deliberate and heavy. All I could think in that moment was that I could not let him near me. I had no other thought except to escape the horror of this man. I turned to the window and jumped. I felt my body falling through the cold air, felt the heavy movement of the wind against me and felt the pull of the rocks beneath me.

In the split-second before hitting the rocks, I moved miraculously out of my body, observing the events with an unbelievable serenity. I watched my body break and bleed upon the rocks. I watched the murderer look down upon my body with obscene satisfaction. I felt no fear, no anguish, just blissful peace, a mere onlooker at my own death, thankfully removed from physical and emotional discomfort.

Then I awoke in my own bed, my heart pounding in fear and pain, my voice howling into the darkness. On opening my eyes, I saw a patch of white light near my bedroom door. I asked if it was my mother but received no answer. The light moved closer. I was immediately immersed in the knowledge that this was my brother, Stephen. I felt bathed in feelings of warmth, love, comfort and absolute peace. I had an overwhelming sense of homecoming. The jolting impact of the nightmare instantly eased. I could not remember ever feeling such complete and satisfying joy.

My brother Stephen had died at the age of six when a gravel truck hit him. My parents had grieved this enormous loss, while acknowledging Stephen's death was part of God's plans. They spent time reassuring the truck driver that they allocated no blame to him for his part in Stephen's death. In their attempts to cope with his death, Stephen's name was no longer mentioned in our home. In the seven years that followed, I had forgotten my brother. This night's visit returned to me the happy memories that I had of our games together. I knew why my brother had come. Every part of me knew. He came to relieve my suffering. And he did.

I never had another nightmare in which I died, or wore a stranger's face or a stranger's body. For this I thank my brother Stephen who, happily, is one of the angels of my life.

Ruth Yanor-McRae

Blue Angel Dress

My father's eldest sister was called Anastasia. In English her name became Mable - not as romantic as Anastasia, more sturdy, functional and strong. She was the matriarch, the keeper of our family history. She shared this often with my father. They would sit late into the night comparing their memories, both sure their version was correct, the way it really happened.

Growing up, I lived in this same community and our families were close. Events in life later caused my aunt to relocate to an urban center where I attended university. I would often visit her and listen to the stories of past days. I would ask questions, sit, drink tea, listen and eat. Always there was food.

When my aunt's son passed on at the young age of fifty-two, there was much sorrow in the family. A few weeks earlier, I had sustained a knee injury requiring major reconstruction. Part of my convalescence was spent at my aunt's home while she was in mourning. I went to physiotherapy, learned to walk again and practised this on her deck. We also spoke of death, the afterlife and how we would tell our loved ones we were okay. We decided to use the colour navy blue.

Many years later, after I had done an initiatory workshop on contacting angels, I walked into my apartment building after a particularly gruelling workday. In the corner of the ceiling, I saw a beautiful aquamarine flash of crystal light. I knew this was my angel letting me know that I was not alone.

A few months later, during a busy workday, I was having

my only quiet moment of the day in the washroom. Suddenly, a navy blue crystalline angel flashed in front of my eyes. "What is this"? I wondered, and "why is it occurring here, of all places"? Later that day at a Reiki energy session, I found the energies were very intense. I felt as if angel wings were brushing my whole body, enfolding me in their loving caresses. They made sure I was aware of their presence.

I arrived home and heard a telephone message telling me that my aunt had died earlier that day. Sorrow filled me, tears coming immediately. Slowly I pieced the signs together. The navy blue angel was my aunt bidding me farewell, giving me the sign of our appointment planned out so many years ago. The angel wings had cleansed my aura and gently caressed me, preparing me for the sad news, yet keeping alive a promise of the angelic realm.

My aunt had always told me in life how good I looked in navy blue. I know beyond a doubt that it was my aunt in the navy blue angel dress. She was showing me a sign of the world beyond.

Linda Malekoff

Sylvia Pinar

Hi-Five Angel

Bill, an elderly, unmarried gentleman, moved into a house across the street from us. He had lived in the area a number of years before, so he came back to live out his last days near his home. We struck up a friendship with him and he became a father figure to my husband, Harold, and myself. He also became an adopted grandfather to our children. We did a number of things together. That year, we invited him to share Christmas with our family. Through tears, he told us that it was the first time he'd had Christmas with anyone in forty years.

As time went on, Bill began to fail. I checked on him regularly, bringing him home cooked meals to make sure he ate properly. By then, we had our own problems.

Harold was diagnosed with colon cancer. One particular trying day, after learning that Harold would need yet another cancer operation, this time in his lungs, I went to check on Bill. He looked at me and said, "Jill, you look so tired. Don't worry about me, I will tell you when I am ready to die."

I thought to myself, 'What is he talking about?'

As we waited for a hospital bed for Harold, Bill became weaker and weaker. His nephew came and moved him in with his family so he and his wife could take care of Bill.

One night after a fitful sleep, I awoke to see Bill standing at the foot of my bed. He appeared healthier than I had seen him for some time. He looked at me, held up his open hand, and said, "Harold will be all right, but I have five days left. Harold will make it but I won't." Then he just faded away.

I sat up with a start and woke Harold. "Did you see Bill?" I cried. "He was just standing at the foot of our bed!" Harold hadn't seen anything.

That evening we went to visit Bill at his nephew's. I talked to his nephew's wife and told her about Bill's visit. I don't think she believed me, but five days later we received a call from Bill's nephew telling us he had passed away.

I thank God every day for sending us this angel who loved us enough to ease our worries and comfort us. Harold's surgery went well and he is home now. Since then, I know that I have an angel looking after me.

As told to Florence Trautman.

Judy Hamilton

Soul Work

My sister was a spirit with a mission. She touched so many people's lives. The ripple effect of who she was and what she did is still felt in so many people's lives - today, and forever.

It is appropriate now that I tell you briefly about my sister. She and I were like Siamese twins. We went through our school years together (grade school, nursing school, and University); we raced together, we sang together, we laughed together - we did everything together. When she died in a car accident at twenty-seven years of age, I went through all the stages of grief. I was angry with God for taking her from me. She was too young. It wasn't fair. She was a lovely, gentle girl and had never hurt others. She simply loved everyone and they her. She lived her mission and in living it, set an example for all those around her. She made a difference! She 'raised the bar'.

Well, one day about a year and a half after her death, when I was 'still', I saw an oval, human shaped light approaching from the distance. I knew instantly that it was the essence, the spirit, of my sister. I hadn't been thinking of her, or praying about her. But this was my Mary! My heart raced. I almost shouted, "Mary!"

She said to me, "Ann, I want you to know something. It was my choice - it was my choice - it was my choice to die - the way I did and when I did, before I ever came down here. I love you."

Instantly, overwhelmed with emotions and tears, I released my pain, my heartache. It was her choice, no one else's. It was her Path. She chose it, not God, not anyone else. It was her choice to live her 'mission' and assist others to walk their Highest Path. Ultimately, when we walk our Highest Path, we are of the 'Universal Divine' and we elevate the energy of the world, the universe.

Ann Keane

Maureen Stefaniuk

Nicotine Angel

Bill and my husband, Ray, worked together at the same job for a number of years and became close friends. The two of them were always laughing and joking around. Then Bill was diagnosed with lung cancer. Both Ray and Bill were long time heavy smokers. As the disease progressed, Bill would plead with Ray, "Stop smoking. Look what it's doing to me."

Ray would reply, "I can't. I've tried but I just can't."

One day after a painfully slow walk, struggling for each breath, Bill came over to our house. He pointed to the house he was having built and said, "See the house I'm building? Where I'm at right now, I'll probably never get to live in it. I'm building it for my wife. Stop smoking, Ray!"

Over the next two and a half years, we visited Bill and his wife often. Each time, Bill would ask Ray to quit smoking. Ray would always reply, "I can't."

When Bill began loosing his battle with the cancer, we visited him again. He reached for Ray's hand and clasped it, speaking softly but with determination. "This is probably the last time I will see you." Then he looked deep into Ray's eyes and continued, "You will quit smoking. You'll see. I'll come and help you."

The next week Bill passed away. After the funeral, Ray went to the refrigerator where he kept his carton of cigarettes and took them out. Eyes full of tears, he dumped the carton in the garbage.

To this day, some twenty years later, Ray has never had a craving for, or even touched a cigarette. More surprisingly, Ray never had any of the symptoms associated with nicotine withdrawal.

Was Bill his angel who came to help him quit smoking? How can we think otherwise?

As told to Florence Trautman

Randall Kabatoff

Kristine's Special Friend

My daughter Kristine is a rambunctious Kindergartner. A few years ago Kristine was diagnosed with ADHD (Attention Deficit Hyperactive Disorder) and some sensitivity problems. We were given a lot of advice on how to deal with her problems but I was becoming very frustrated.

The woman I worked for at the time was a Reiki Master. She suggested that a session might help Kristine. We arrived at her studio and Kristine immediately calmed down and stopped fidgeting. The room was beautifully decorated with angels. Soft, soothing music played and candles burned around the room. As my boss performed the Reiki, Kristine, who also had some kidney problems, immediately had to go to the washroom down the hall.

Afterwards, Kristine ran back calling, "There is a man floating in the hall!'

Both my boss and I rushed into the hall but no one was there. The amazing thing was that all the doors were locked and we were the only ones in the building.

Although I have no idea what he was there for, I do believe that Kristine saw 'a floating man'. This isn't the first time that she has seen something. My son Jared, Kristine's brother, passed away when she was ten months old. Although she has seen pictures of him and heard stories, she would have no memories of her own. However, on several occasions she has told me things about Jared. She has had talks with him and even plays with him.

There is no doubt in my mind that Jared is Kristine's guardian angel.

Sherri Jacklin

Visit With a Very Special Angel

About four years ago, when I was eighteen, I had an experience that changed my beliefs about angels and life after death. When my dad was a little boy, my grandma had a baby named Craig. He was with them for only a short time before passing away while still a baby. I thought about him quite often and wondered what he would be like. What would he look like? Then all my questions were answered.

One night, while sleeping, I had a vision. A wonderful vision indeed. I saw a very bright, white light shining towards me and a man walked through it. He was wearing a blue windbreaker, a grey T-shirt, blue jeans and running shoes. Neatest of all, he seemed familiar. He had dark, black hair and looked like my dad and his younger brother. He was so peaceful looking and so kind, I wasn't scared. It was such a wonderful spiritual feeling and I felt so safe with him. His words were simple but held great meaning for me. He said, "Hi, I'm your Uncle Craig. I'm okay and everything is going to be all right."

These were special words from a special man. I know now that I have an angel on my shoulder. In fact, when I was a very small baby, I almost left the world not once, but twice due to an illness. I think that Uncle Craig was the one who pulled me through it. I have a destiny in this life and he's making sure, by being my angel, that it is fulfilled.

I will never forget that night and the warm feeling I had. I will always be looking over my shoulder.

Shandra Kim Davies

My Friend Joan, My Spirit Guide

It was the spring of 1996. My family and I had lived through the winter, watching helplessly as my mother's health continued to fail. Cancer had attacked her body and finally, in April, it took its toll on her. During this time I was totally preoccupied with my mother's well being. Consequently, I neglected my friends. I visited them only for short periods, often by phone, keeping my conversations brief and to the point.

My friend Joan, a tall, slim, English lady was one of these friends. She was quick tempered, quick tongued and never believed in 'clouding' anything. She was always very direct and expected you to be the same. Joan had a big heart and if you were her friend, she would do anything for you.

I met her twenty-three years ago and she was my friend from that moment on. Through the years we shared many things. We laughed together, cried together and felt each other's pain. We were always there to help each other out through the rough times.

Joan always shared her knowledge with me. Her life was filled with experiences. She was a great photographer, wrote poetry, and loved to read. She spent countless hours reading many types of fiction including romance novels, mysteries and autobiographies. These she read with an open mind, often questioning her findings. Many times she discussed them with me. Her recent passion was reading books on heavenly encounters. She read about life after death, angel encounters and travelling to heaven or the 'next plane'.

Joan often spoke of spirit guides and heavenly presences

that she felt as a breeze blowing by her when she was indoors. One time, we watched as doors down the hallway banged closed and a cold breeze blew by us. She could feel a touch by someone who was not visible to the naked eye. Joan also told me about the clanking footsteps that she heard. She claimed it was her friend from the past, walking past her room and down the stairs. She would say, "Those little wooden heeled, pink slippers could be heard throughout the building."

You might say that Joan was in touch with the 'other plane'. Her dream of ships sailing into a harbour always amazed me. She said she would stand helplessly on the pier as these ships with a date written on the side lined up for people to board them. Beside her stood a lady with a bright light shining behind her. Joan talked about standing on the pier watching her father board a ship and wave goodbye to her saying, 'No Joan you cannot come, it is not your time yet." She told me of her shock when her father passed away on the very date that was written on the side of the ship. Then she had another dream. This time, her mother boarded the ship with the date on it and once again she passed away on the same day that was written on the side of the ship.

Then one day Joan came to me and said, "Jacquie, my ship came into port last night. I couldn't see the date but I got on board and waved to you on the shore. I think I may die soon."

My mother was ill, I had no time to consider this. I passed it off as a bad dream. Two weeks after my mother's death, the phone rang before dawn. It was Joan, panic-stricken, "I can't breathe!" she gasped.

Fearing the worst, I raced to her apartment and found her gasping for breath, her face blue. It was a long trip to the hospital and I hoped that my inner feelings were wrong.

Joan said, "You know Jacquie, I'm going to die. I will not come home. I am not afraid to die." And I knew what she said was true. Suddenly she said, "How are you going to be without me, Jacquie?" I told her not to worry about me but to put her energy into herself.

Still, this concern did not leave her. During the next few weeks we became closer than ever before. We talked about our past, our lives, our memories and we shared secrets with one another.

Joan was diagnosed with cancer of the liver, brain and lungs, which spread rapidly, leaving her unable to walk or care for herself. One day as I came through the door, she looked up at me with a smile and asked, "Did you meet the Australian man"? I looked at her, puzzled, and replied that I had not seen him. Joan continued, "I know you think that I am on morphine and Atian but I am thinking clearly right now and I did talk to him. He was wearing a long oil slicker coat and a brimmed hat. We had a long talk."

Joan was quite matter of fact about her condition. "I have to die. Don't be upset, Jacquie, for I do love you, my friend. I have to die so I can be your spirit guide. You looked after me always, now I must look after you."

I could not accept this. Tears streaming down my face; I hugged her frail body, wanting to sob in her neck. She continued to comfort me, "Oh, Jacquie, please don't cry, I'll always be by your side. I will help you, just ask when you need me."

Joan slipped into a coma a few hours later. Her ship had arrived. Within a few days, she passed away.

Then things began to happen. I felt her presence imme-diately. She came home with me from the hospital, but I passed it off. I reasoned that it was because she had been so close to me. But that was far from the truth. I felt her presence at the memorial service and knew that she was proud of her service.

After the funeral, I was sitting alone in my living room when I felt a touch on my arm. I thought it was a fly and brushed it away, then it came again, like a fingertip. I remembered that Joan used to touch me like that when she passed by me. Then I smelled a freshly lit cigarette behind me. Joan had been a chain smoker. Instantly, I knew that she was giving me a sign. From that day on, all I have to do is call on Joan if I am in trouble or if I need to find something and she is there to help me. It takes a moment and the thing I lost will appear or I will be guided to find it. In fact, Joan's co-workers can also ask her for help.

It has been four years since Joan passed away but she is a very busy spirit. She has helped many people find special items like an heirloom brooch lost in a Saan Store and a grieving son's only momento of his deceased father: his legionnaire hats. The son had searched his entire house and found nothing. Joan told him to look in the third suitcase in the attic and there they were! One cold night, she even started my stalled car while I helplessly stood in front of it with the hood raised.

How fortunate I am to have had a good friend here on earth and now a friend in the spiritual world. Thanks, Joan.

Jacqueline Cunningham

This story was chosen as best story, of the *HeartBeat Angels* story contest, because Jacqueline knew her spiritual guide, Joan, before Joan died ... and knew that she would be a guide.

Randall Kabatoff

CHAPTER 4

Sun and Cloud Visions

*"A great sign appeared in the sky,
a woman clothed with the sun".*
Revelations 12: 1

Powerful messages have been received by "seers" viewing clouds and the sun. The sun, in particular, has been appearing in various forms and colours. "Evidence in Marmora, Ontario, Canada, reveals the miracle of the sun which has been seen countless times by thousands of people from more than twenty countries", writes Sister Alice Johnson. "The individual may look directly into the sun for upwards of twenty minutes without damage to one's eyes. The sun discs over with a gorgeous shade of blue-green, becomes encircled with breath-taking rainbow colours, spins, then throbs in such a way as to make one's heart beat in union with the heartbeat of the universe. Some people see images in the sun ... Jesus, Mary, the Cross, a dove ... and are profoundly moved by the vision which touches their soul at a deep level. It is an awesome experience". This same sun is stunning people all over the world. Why not view it for yourself?

Randall Kabatoff

A Photographer's Vision Images

$\mathbf{M}$y childhood love of nature has turned into a career as a photographer and for over 20 years my most common subject is nature's beauty. I feel privileged to see some of the visions nature has to offer and I feel my photographs are meant to be shared and enjoyed with others. Often I describe myself as a spiritual bridge builder between nature and the viewer of the photograph.

For the last eight years I have been interested in the spiritual aspects of photography. I believe I am guided to photograph certain scenes and I believe that spirit plays a role in composing the scene. I often discover that when I create a photograph there are sometimes images in the picture that I was not conscious of when I pressed the shutter button. Now, more than ever, I believe creative photography is more accurately a co-creative spiritual process since the images are a product of the conscious mind, the unconscious mind and the spiritual mind. I believe the same is true for all creative art forms.

Visionary artist Alex Grey says art's highest and original meaning is the subjective revelation of spirit. When a photographer, or other creative artist, is awake to the spiritual landscape they can represent this terrain in an artistic way through their medium.

The picture of the Aborginal elder on the previous page is a case in point. My friend, Grandma Grizzly, was praying when I took this picture, and she was asking for direction to a question. I took the slide of this portrait and I was inspired to get a cloud picture from my slide collection to superimpose over her picture. The combined effect is what you see. Some time later a child pointed to the cloud that looks like an angel in exactly the spot that the elder is gazing up to. The "angel cloud" also mirrors the out stretched arms of the elder. To all the amazed people who have since seen this image, there is a sense that spiritual serendipity played a role in this. To Grandma Grizzly the angel cloud was an answer to her question.

I am dedicated to the creation of images that inspire the spirit and evoke the questions in the viewers ongoing journey of greater spiritual understanding. In the picture below I sought to portray this woman's light in her heart area. I selected a sunset from my slide collection and superimposed it over her portrait. It was later pointed out to me by a viewer that by placing this sunset here it alligned the cloud over her right shoulder to her wing position. She has an eagle feather over one shoulder and an angel wing on the other shoulder.

I pray that I may continue to work with spirit co-creatively.

Randall Kabatoff

Randall Kabatoff

A Cloud of Trust

My mom was the kindest, most understanding person I have ever known. We were very close. Each knew what the other was thinking as we laughed and cried together. Our house was always full, with seven kids plus the many relatives and friends who came to visit. Mom made room for everyone with her welcome smile. Her patience was endless. When she was very ill and dying, it was hard to understand why someone so good had to suffer so terribly. After about six months in the hospital, mom died in pain that could not be controlled by medication.

I was very bitter and terribly upset by her death. I could not understand why she had to suffer, why she had to die and leave me. About two months after her death, I was thinking about mom when I began to feel very weepy. I started questioning my faith. I remembered that mom always had so much faith but I didn't seem to have any.

Living in the country gives me time to think for twenty minutes while driving back and forth to work. On this particular summer morning, I was on the main highway when I looked up at the sky with tears in my eyes, my mind full of questions. There before me was a perfect cross. It looked like it was made by a jet stream. I pulled over to the side of the road and got out to look for a plane. There was none in sight. I knew instantly that it was my mom's way of letting me know she was indeed among angels and to keep my faith.

I did keep my faith and my belief in angels has increased. I started making angels of every size and shape, then gave courses to teach others how to make them for themselves. I even went further. I opened up my own shop with my daughter. Yes, it is full of angels and we are both having fun learning the business and learning about each other. It is such a wonderful thought that my mom is among the real angels in heaven.

Mary Brown

Janine Balser

Clouds of Angels

When I was eight years old, my brother and I were visiting my grandparents in St. Paul, Alberta, Canada. We were going to my grandmother's school reunion. My brother and I were sitting in the back seat of the car. He was sitting behind my grandfather and I was sitting behind my grandmother. I looked out my side of the car window and I saw clouds that looked interesting. Suddenly, I realized that these clouds looked like angels. The first one had a face with eyes, nose and mouth. The hair was flowing in the breeze. Even though I don't remember too much about her gown, I remember she had one. The second angel was sitting on a stool playing the harp. Her face had no features because she was sitting sideways. I was very excited and asked my brother if he could see them and he said, "No." I kept on pointing to the clouds but he could not see them. I did not tell anyone about this until now.

Rebecca Newman

Age 8

Rebecca Newman

Colours in the Sky

I was in the car with my grandparents. I was sitting in the back seat. We were just talking and I looked up at the sun. It was turning different colours and was spinning around. It was orange, yellow, bluish-green, then red and pink. We looked at it for a while. Then we went home. On the way home we were going away from the sun but I could still see the sun's circles with many different colours in the sky. The sun was behind me but I could see circles in front of me too. It was neat.

Alexander Hruschuk

Age 8

The Colourful Sun

I was going to the Main Street Garage Sale with my grandmother and sister. I was sitting in the back seat of the car. I looked up at the sun and it was so bright! Then I saw the sun turn many different colours. It turned yellow, blue, green, purple and white like a light bulb. I told my grandmother and we stopped the car to watch it. The sun began to spiral round and round. It was so bright that we put our hands over our eyes and just peeked through our fingers. We moved to the shadow of the trees and the sun came right through the trees. It was so cool to watch as the angels were playing games.

Matthew Newman

Age 6

Eyes in the Sky

It was mid-August, 1994, a beautiful day with blue skies and warm summer breezes. How happy I felt inside. For several years now, I have been on a spiritual quest, searching for an inner peace that I occasionally achieve. I started my car and headed west, feeling so excited for some reason. It was the type of excitement I feel when I am going somewhere special and can hardly wait to get there. Yet I wasn't going anywhere in particular, just home after a day's work.

I have always been a cloud watcher. As a small girl, I remember looking at the cloud shapes and seeing animals of various sizes; later it was angels or just their wings. Once, I even saw a cloud formed like a cross and another like a church. Watching cloud formations amuses and relaxes me during the twenty-minute drive to and from work. It is great fun, a game I play with my angels.

On this particular day, however, there wasn't a cloud to be seen as I approached the main highway. I couldn't remember a bright sunny day without even a tiny cloud to gaze upon. Then suddenly an oval cloud appeared to my right; it looked like an oval donut. "How strange to be in such perfect formation," I thought. Then it opened up larger with so much depth that I caught my breath.

I heard a voice saying, "Look to the left." I turned my head slowly and felt something grab my stirring wheel. I knew I was no longer in control of my car but I wasn't concerned. I felt very uplifted and fascinated by the two clouds that began to form, coming closer and clearer. My heart raced as I realized that they were two eyes in perfect detail: the veins, the irises and the pupils - all there in the blue sky - exquisitely formed. "It can't be!" I thought. "If they were eyes there would be a nose." Sure enough, along came a paintbrush and gave me a nose. Yet the nose didn't match the perfect artwork of the eyes. I could hear a whisper, "there is your nose." What a beauty in the sky! For an instant I thought about pulling over to take a better look, but I knew someone else was taking care of my car so I just focused on the sky. I was afraid that the heavenly eyes would disappear.

"What does this mean?" I thought. "Could it mean I was going to die? No, I didn't think I was about to die. Could it be for someone else?"

No, these eyes were meant for me and they were the eyes of Jesus. "Why?" I asked. Instantly I knew that this was my reward for working so hard on my spirituality. I was spellbound though my brain denied my vision, filling my head with doubts and questions. Then, the eyes disappeared. It seemed like the vision lasted for several minutes but I'm sure it was only seconds. I came back to reality and began shivering uncontrollably as I pulled onto a side road. I can't find words to explain my astonishment and awe. I began to cry, filled with a powerful joy and excitement similar to what I experienced at the birth of my grandchildren. This was like a new birth for me.

This experience widened the doorway to the spiritual realm for me. It was an affirmation, an unforgettable one. The vivid impression stays with me, bringing a comforting peace that I have sought for so long. My enlightenment and expansion continues daily. And still I watch every cloud formation for more surprises.

Pauline Newman

Miracle of the Sun

My initial awareness began in 1999. The sun was appearing in different colours and, at times, a very intense strength would begin a pulsing effect. At first, the sun appeared to filter through the trees, then it would completely absorb the trees, as if they weren't there. This was so incredible and I began sharing this experience with friends. However, they could not see anything.

It wasn't until 2000 that I actually began to experience changes within myself when I viewed this phenomena. This brilliant, gleaming sun made my heart race and tumble, a new heart beat. What was it? I was so fascinated, mesmerized, yet excited as I began to study this physical evidence more closely. Intuition told me that there was more to be discovered but no information was available.

July to September 2000 was the most intense time for me. My grandchildren also experienced this mystical moment. They are kindred spirits and open-minded. Sometimes we would have humorous conversations as to the reasoning of this manifestation. Their lives are full of synchronistic events and coincidences that adults take for granted. Life for them is about joy of the moment and the sun could be telling grandma to give them a treat. Another said it was for good luck.

I began once again to share this visual occurrence with other insight seekers. Some saw the rainbow around the sun. Some were too busy to look. Others didn't trust the sun because of the strong effect on the eyes. I couldn't find anyone who was as excited as I was.

The sun was game playing with me, each time giving me a new experience. At times there was a rainbow around the perimeter, then changes of various colours, which went into a spinning motion. The colours changed from orange to red then green to blue and, perhaps, a translucent white before disking across the sky.

Looking out my kitchen window one evening, I saw the shape of the sun form into a heart. "This is unbelievable", I exclaimed to my husband who thought the sun was too bright to look at. Seeing this event made me feel very happy.

While in conscious meditation, I asked God for guidance about this mystery. I wanted more clarity. Now it came to pass, while I shopped in our local St. Francis Centre, when a prayer card, *"Our Lady of Light"*, appeared in my purchase bag. This was my first clue as I read the brief history of the happenings in Kentucky, U.S.A. I returned to the store for more cards to give to friends but was told that they did not know where it came from and that it was not from their religious centre. Now I was on to something, something big.

On October 19, 2000, my grandson, Ryan's third birthday, I had my most incredible vision of the sun's dancing miracle on my way to work. Immediately I phoned the number on the prayer card and spoke to a delightful lady, Margaret O'Conner, who filled me in on the 1991 visionary beginnings in Ohio and Kentucky. Margaret and I began a long distance friendship as I shared my excitement and profound soul connection to the sun. We spoke of adversaries and negative responses that her group had overcome. Graciously, she helped submit three stories that appear in the Miracles From Powerful Prayers chapter. She told me that the sun appears on the eighth day of the month while giving messages for visionaries from Mary, the mother of Jesus, and from Jesus himself.

The next month I heard about the miracle sun happening in Marmora, Ontario, Canada. With the help from St.

Joseph's Bookstore, I was able to obtain a used book, "Marmora Canada: Is Our Blessed Mother Speaking Here to Her Beloved Children?", written by Sister Alice Johnson. Sister Alice and I also became long distance friends. While I wasn't able to publish them in this *HeartBeat Angels* book, they will be in the next book. Sister Alice did write commentaries in several chapters.

Sister Alice told about rosary chains turning colour, miracle healings, and visions of angels, which often take place on the first Saturday of the month.

On March 3, 2001, I was at a retreat house. After the Stations of the Cross prayers, I lingered behind in the Grotto. I noticed another lady there and gave her one of *"Our Lady of Light"* prayer cards. With a sudden explosion, the sun began it's miraculous show. Nettie, from Valleyview, Alberta introduced herself and explained that she had visited Medjugorje, Yugoslavia three times, where she witnessed the same phenomena, including the cross, the spinning and the colours. Our only comments were "Look, look!" The sun performed for us for nearly half an hour before showering us with a golden yellow light, completely covering us. The dazzling effects gave us a sense of peace, hope and nearness to our Lord.

Not only is the sun displaying these miracles, but the moon also appears with the rainbow, spiralling and changing colours. These have been witnessed by myself, and several friends, in December, 2000.

By now *HeartBeat Angels* is ready for print. Listening to my angels, I was guided to share this manifestation. More of these stories will be written in Book Two. Because it has been a unique privilege for me to have a glimpse into what may be the greatest miracle of this century, I want to share it with you. Perhaps you, too, can lift your head to the heavens for your own connection. God Bless.

Pauline Newman

Michael Godet – based on a vision of Douglas Severight

CHAPTER 5

Spiritual Visions

*"Suddenly the skies burst into brilliant Light
and an angel appeared".*
Luke 2:15

We often think of angels
with wings or with a glowing bright light. Yet, if we look
beyond our physical eyes to other supernatural phenomena, we find that we can see beyond our five senses.
Musicians, such as Beethoven, received their inspiration
when they heard Divine music. With this in mind, can
we receive spiritual messages from animals, unexplainable and powerful sensory smells or are there angels pos-
ing as humans in order to help understand God's mysterious creation? When such an event occurs we are left in
a stupor, confused, yet filled with divine warmth and
inspiration. If we limit our boundaries to our five senses,
it leads us to a scientific material world. However, we
must not neglect the invisible wisdom of the Creator.

Randall Kabatoff

The Eagle is With Me

It was many years ago when I first became aware of the eagle coming to comfort me. My marriage was quickly deteriorating. I was at the end of my rope, unsure how much longer I could hang on. We had been married for twenty-five years. Up to that point, I had never considered leaving. After all, I took my vows seriously and thought I could tough it out. I had to consider my children, though adults and on their own by then, plus the repercussions from family and community.

One year earlier, I had taken a course on Therapeutic Touch. I helped many people with my energy work. They began coming to my home for healing. That, too, became more and more difficult because I didn't feel I had enough knowledge but didn't know what to do about it. Yet I always understood that what happened was not of my doing. I was but an instrument of something much bigger. Whenever people asked questions, I always replied, "It's a mystery."

My husband would often meet people at the door, even before they had entered, and he would tell them, "I don't believe in all that stuff." He questioned me day and night but I could not provide any answers that satisfied him. I knew so little.

I was truly unhappy about the dilemma I faced. But at the same time, my work with other people gave me such satisfaction. Each experience was so sacred I still can not find the words to express it.

One evening we were driving home through the countryside. It was a beautiful winter night with stars sparkling across the dark sky. A full moon shone down.

Yet my heart felt so heavy. Inside, I cried out for help.

Suddenly, in front of us appeared a giant translucent eagle. It was about six feet from wingtip to wingtip, its color a soft gold. Then I realized it was sitting behind me and wrapping me with its wings. Never have I felt such love, such peace. Tears rolled down my face, tears of emotions that I had no understanding about - not then. Nevertheless, from that moment on, I knew that I was looked after, that I would receive guidance and healing and most of all, that I could trust in God, the Great Creator.

A few years later, I received a traditional name from an Aboriginal Elder. He would later become my husband.

My name is Eagle Woman.

Randall Kabatoff

Stranger on the Bus

It was a dreary February. At fifty-five, Mom lay ravaged with cancer in her home in Portage, Manitoba, Canada. My father had quit his job to be with her. My sister and brothers were also there. My husband and I had been transferred to Hinton, Alberta, Canada the previous year. In November, I traveled by train to visit, reminisce, make peace, express my love and just to be with Mom while at the same time helping Dad out.

The dreaded phone call came late one night. It was time to go home once again. Mom didn't have much time left.

We were a young couple with young children trying to make ends meet. I worked as a florist and made arrangements with my employer for a salary advance to purchase a bus ticket (God bless my boss). My husband was out of town on business so I hired a baby-sitter until he returned. He and the children would later drive to Portage once arrangements could be made for the funeral.

The bus trip was long with numerous stops along the way. One stop I will never forget was in Edmonton, Alberta. There was an hour layover and I had to change buses. While boarding the bus, I noticed a tall, stately built African American man getting on the bus. I was in such a miserable and desperate state that it is a wonder I noticed this man at all, as he seated himself across the aisle from me. Immediately, a feeling of peace came over me. Throughout the trip I prayed, using my rosary, holding it down and hiding it from others. Tears came now and then with all my memories. I felt his eyes gently gazing towards me as he turned his head ever so slowly. Instantly, I felt lifted up spiritually and filled with peace. Each time the bus stopped for breaks, he would follow me at a close distance, sitting near me, comforting me with his presence but never speaking.

We were due to arrive in Portage at 6:00 a.m. I prayed continually. By 3:00 a.m. that morning, I heard the words, "I'm okay, don't pray for me, pray for the rest." At that moment, I knew my dear mother was at peace at last.

We arrived in Portage on time and my aunts and cousins were waiting for me. My first words to them were, "She died, didn't she?" My aunt asked how I had known. I relayed the events of the trip to my relatives as they stood in silence, believing what I told them.

The bus made two stops in Portage. The first one was where I departed, and the second one was at a coffee shop for a break. I was the only passenger who got off at the first stop. Approaching the car, my aunt explained that my dad had not had much sleep but finally fell asleep just before they left to pick me up. She suggested that we go to the coffee shop and let him sleep. Our conversation would wake him up.

We followed the bus to the coffee shop where everyone got out and we went into the shop for a snack. I looked for my African American friend but he wasn't in the coffee shop. My cousin and I both went to the bus looking for him but he wasn't on the bus either. I believed instinctively that he was an angel sent from God to console, comfort and strengthen me for what lay ahead.

At the time, I didn't think too much about the gentleman's apparel. He wore dark pants, and a light coloured shirt with neither overcoat nor luggage. Now that I think about how cold the month of February is in Alberta, I wonder why I never noticed how strangely he was dressed.

My attraction with angels has remained throughout my life, more so now that I am a grandmother. Whenever I am in need of spiritual guidance, I am often attracted to people with the same connection whether it be at a flee market, at my place of employment or with certain neighbours. My trust in God and the angels is very strong and forever present as my spirituality increases. I thank God for this treasure.

Kathy Johnston

Randall Kabatoff

The Rabbit

Several years ago, my eight year old son passed away in a swimming accident. Anyone who has lost a loved one knows how devastating this is. You try to make sense of it, try to rationalize it, even try to deny it. Along with all the emotions, you try to get some comfort and peace of mind.

One particular day, I was having a very hard time coping. Although I believed my son was in a better place, as a mother I had a hard time with it. So many questions crossed my mind, some silly, some reasonable. Was he warm enough? Was he scared? Could he see us and know how much we missed him? Was heaven beautiful? Was he lonely? I prayed so hard for some sign that would give me a small measure of comfort. •

The next day, my husband and I went to the cemetery. When we approached my son's grave, there, sitting calmly looking around, were two lovely wild rabbits. They didn't turn and run away, as I first expected, but let us come quite close. One turned and, I swear, gave me the most incredible look. In that instant I knew this was my sign that my son was okay and not alone.

You see, my son used to love to run out in the field by his grandma's house in the hopes of catching a rabbit. He would try and try, of course without success. He was also born in the Chinese Year of the Rabbit.

Although a rabbit is not how I envisioned an angel to look, there's no doubt in my mind that those two rabbits were angels sent down to give me peace of mind.

Oh, by the way, whenever I'm having a particularly hard day, I can guarantee that when I go to the cemetery, the rabbits will still be there.

Sherri Jacklin

Sherri won the second prize in the *HeartBeat Angels* story competition.

Frank Burman

Visitor in the Park

I remember vividly the day I met an angel in the park. At the time, I wasn't aware that she might have been an angel.

I was a teenager, growing up in central British Columbia, Canada. My mother became sick, very sick, and I knew she was dying. When she ended up in the hospital, I refused to go see her. My dad did everything in his power to coax me to visit her but I refused adamantly. I was only a teenager and my mother was dying. I felt she was abandoning me, betraying me by being so sick. Parents are supposed to look after us, not die. Eventually, my father gave up asking me.

One day, however, as I sat in school, thoughts of my mom kept coming up, so much so that I gathered up my books and other belongings and went to the hospital. When I got to the hospital, I was once again grief stricken and could not go in. There was a park across from the hospital so I decided I could go there and work up enough nerve to actually go and see mom.

As I sat there, an old lady, probably in her seventies, came dancing across the lawn. She was so full of life for an older person that I was taken by her gestures. She sat down beside me on the bench. I did not know her but she began speaking to me, asking why I was sitting alone. Suddenly, I poured out my heart to this stranger. I sobbed through most of the conversation. When I finished, she asked how I would feel if I never had a chance to make a connection, express my feelings and say goodbye. I knew she was right so I thanked her, wiped my eyes and reached down for my purse. When I looked up, she was gone.

I went into my mother's hospital room to make the connection that I knew I had to make. Mom and I did make up and I found the peace I was looking for.

Later, I kept thinking about the lady in the park and about what she had told me. I made a promise to myself that if I ever saw her again, I would thank her for helping me see the truth. I kept looking around for her everywhere. One day while entering a downtown restaurant, I spotted her. I decided to buy her a coffee since she was sitting alone at a table. I approached her, delighted at my find, placing the cup of coffee in front of her. I began expressing my feelings of gratitude, thanking her for her comforting words that day in the park and for helping me see how wrong I was. Suddenly, reality hit me when she said, "I was never at that park."

Dumbfounded, I felt a chill run through my spine. The lady looked at me with all sincerity and I knew she was telling the truth. I also knew instinctively that my visitor in the park was not from this earthly plane.

My mother died about two months later and my life somehow changed since that visit in the park. I always was intuitive but never trusted it. With this new affirmation, I began listening to my heart and trusting myself.

Now, twenty years later, I let things go around me rather than through me. I also know that if you don't settle your differences between loved ones, you will carry those differences for the rest of your life. It is better to make peace than carry those regrets. I'm happy that God sent me an angel and that I learned to make peace with my mom.

Tricia Raphael

Room Full of Flowers

My mother, Clara Bush, came from Moon Lake, Alberta, Canada. When her illness struck, she moved to Edmonton, closer to her children and the hospital. For the last five years she had suffered from emphysema and was on oxygen.

In the spring of 2000, she was asleep when a strong fragrance woke her. As she became more awake she was surprised at how powerful the smell was. Yes, it definitely was the smell of flowers. Mom never slept with the light on so the room was dark. Slowly she lifted her head to see where the smell came from. She couldn't recall having any flowers in her room. Sitting up, she gazed upon a room full of flowers. Flowers were everywhere. This was beyond belief! Where did they come from? There were flowers of every kind, colour and shape - like something in a movie but not in her bedroom.

Mom was always a witty person and she had all her faculties about her. She knew that these were powerful smelling flowers. They eventually disappeared but their fragrance remained for a little while before she went back to sleep.

Mom told all of us this story many times before passing away in June 2000. She believed in and read the Bible. I would say that she was close to God. None of us could figure out why she had a vision of a room full of flowers with such a strong smell.

Our family was to undergo much sorrow as we buried four family members, including Mom, all within a five-month period. Was this a memory for us to cling to in our sorrow? Was this to remind us that we are special in God's eyes? Our mother must have been very special to have such a vision. Now, whenever I smell flowers, I think of my mother.

Pat Turner

Randall Kabatoff

Have You Seen an Angel?

One of the first Health Shows our group participated in was The Health Expo, a three-day event in November, 1994, in Edmonton, Alberta, Canada.

The trade fair section was very diverse and to say the least, unusual. Local television stations ITV and CFRN gave each participant a two-minute Info-mercial, an informative commercial for advertising. The fair co-ordinator had financial commitments so there were many different displays. Workshops covered subjects from financial prosperity to fine tuning electric guitars.

Our group, Institute for Therapeutic Touch and Holistic Healing Modalities, were present to create awareness of a holistic approach to healing and education in the healing arts. We offered newsletters, free Therapeutic Touch™, Reflexology and gentle massage. We also had Angel Messenger Cards for people to shuffle and choose their personal written messages from.

At the start, the crowds were very small. People quickly went around the displays and back out the door. The second day didn't improve matters. Finally Sunday arrived and it appeared that this venue wasn't a good one financially or for networking options.

Tami, a close friend, had volunteered to help me for the weekend. We chatted about the event and took down information from those interested in joining our group. Most people were not too interested but we did see college students signing up for the guitar workshop.

Sunday afternoon, a strange occurrence came about.

Tami and I noticed the shift in our audience when three young women came to our table to look at the Angel cards. The trio were most unusual in their dress; nothing seemed to fit or match in colour. The young ladies were between 14 and 17 years of age. One was bald with a cute slouch hat, another had a weird fake fur coat and tattered jeans, the third had striped tights, shorts, earmuffs and a scarf. They didn't look like typical teenagers. They were, however, excited about the Angel Messenger Cards. I told them about a Women's Festival I had been in and they wanted more information so I gave them phone numbers. Suddenly, they disappeared!

When Tami and I sat down to discuss what had just happened, our table was encased in complete quiet peace. We both looked around to see where the trio had gone but they were nowhere in sight. The room was not crowded so Tami decided to do a complete walk around to see if she could find them. When she returned, she handed me her note and assumption: 'Angels in Training'. They were checking us out to see if we were legit. I believe it.

How about you, seen any Angels lately?

L.M. Woznica

Was the Butterfly an Angel?

Wendy and I had a very close, loving relationship through our many years together, raising our three children. Then, just two days before our twenty-seventh anniversary, she was gone. A blood clot in her lungs took her from me. Victim services arrived almost immediately, offering an invaluable service, making arrangements and just knowing who to contact. I simply could not comprehend what was happening, or why.

Only the day before, as my partner and I patrolled the highways in our farming community, we had discussed how hard it would be to manage without our wives. Now I was living it. My life would never be the same.

The next few days blended into a haze of activity. The memorial service was a blur of people giving condolences and wishing the children and me well. Later, Rita, Wendy's cleaning lady, catered the interment service. How would I ever go on without Wendy?

A few weeks later, Rita came to the house to do the regular house cleaning. I began talking to her about coping with the loss of someone so dear. I knew she would understand because she had tragically lost not one, but two husbands. We talked about feelings and coping with loss of a loved one. I found her easy to talk to and we talked for hours. Over the next few months, Rita helped me through the unfolding process of grief and the endless feelings of emptiness. Through it all, we developed a steady friendship.

Although I had overcome much, one place still weighed on my mind that I seemed afraid to face. It was the family's favourite vacation spot on Shuswap Lake, British Columbia, Canada. We called it our "Hawaii in Canada". I asked Rita to join me in visiting the lake, hoping it might repair my aching spirit. We went there in late fall.

As Rita and I walked along the beach talking, I let the fresh breeze calm my troubled thoughts. Along the way, I mentioned to Rita that I could not see any insects or bugs of any kind along the beach - how curious. We came back from our walk and sat on a bench near my favourite tree where Wendy and I had always put our blanket on the beach.

As we sat on the bench, memories of the wonderful times Wendy and I shared on this spot flooded my mind. My eyes became bubbling fountains as waves of grief shook my body. Rita put her arms around me, sharing my sorrow. She felt my pain and understood. After a time I leaned back on the bench with a deep broken sigh, giving a rest to my eyes, weary of tears. As I looked across the lake, a large orange and brown butterfly, with a wing span of about four inches, came from somewhere behind me and fluttered in front of me. It finally rested on my chest, in my heart area. It sat there for a few seconds and then flew, landing on the very spot Wendy and I always put our beach blanket. As I stared at the butterfly, a warm glow of calmness, peace, serenity and meaning transcended my being. I breathed in the essence of the beautiful moment, capturing it in my memory. With a sense of wonderment and divinity, I looked at Rita and asked, "Are you thinking what I'm thinking?" Rita nodded. I wondered if Wendy was really saying, "I'm all right. Your love is not lost; it flows back to heal your heart. It's time for you to move on with your life."

I do not know what the real meaning was, but I do know that I will always savour that special moment and special place and remember it as a charming garden that started my heart blooming again. It made flowers grow out of dark memories. I now know that happiness requires hope, faith and a willingness to move on when faced with change. I know my life is sweeter because I shared those years with Wendy. I also know that since that moment, I have come to terms with my loss and am ready to move on, thanks to a butterfly.

As told to Florence Trautman

Randall Kabatoff

Mexican Vacation

My husband Philip and I own and operate the St. Joseph and Angels Catholic Bookstore in Edmonton, Alberta, Canada. In the days before we opened the store, we spent a lot of time traveling across Canada and the United States. One of our most interesting trips was the one to Mexico City. Before leaving, we had checked with the Mexican Consulate who warned us that Mexico had a lot of bad press about bandits. We resolved to be careful.

Driving back from Mexico, we reached a town called Matamoros. We were having a hard time finding the Mexican/American border. Several people we stopped to ask replied, "Speak no English!" Stopped at a red light, we noticed the car beside us had an English 'For Sale,' sign on it so I rolled down my window and asked the driver how to get to the border.

He called back, "Follow me! I will take you there!"

After following him for several minutes through the downtown, my husband felt that we were being taken on a 'scenic tour' of the city. He was afraid that if we didn't come to the border soon, we might lose the car. At that moment, the driver ahead of us pointed out the border. When my husband turned to wave a 'thank you', the car disappeared into thin air!

Janet MacLellan

Ashlee Moser

CHAPTER 6

Children's Stories

"Truly I tell you, unless you change and become like children, you will never enter the kingdom of heaven. Whoever becomes humble like this child is the greatest in the kingdom of heaven".
Matthew 18:3

Children are close to God because they have just arrived from the spiritual world. With their innocence and openness, they are very intuitive and more receptive than adults with worldly taboos. The angelic kingdom inspires children daily to experience the true magic of self-knowledge and awareness. A child's 'pretend' world is a perspective of trust and love. Unfortunately, not all adults believe the whisper of little children and not every child relates their divine experience. Often, you will notice in adults that the heart, with its intuition, will tell you one thing, while the mind pipes in with reasons as to why this may not be the truth. Children do not experience this as readily. Their belief in honesty creates a world of things visible and invisible.

Chelsi Cunningham

Deanie

My name is Chelsi Cunningham. At this time, I am 10 years old and I see angels. Angels have always been an important part of my life. When I was about two years old I first met my friend Deanie.

Deanie was a very strange looking boy. He had green hair and red teeth. I told my mom and dad about Deanie. They thought he was an imaginary friend but I knew he was an angel and he was very real to me.

Deanie was always at my side. He stayed with me through the good and the bad times. At age 6, my special grandma died. After she died, Deanie let my grandma look after me. Deanie moved to China.

My grandma has come to visit me every day since I was six years old. She talks about my mom and auntie and about the things they did.

I tell my mom what grandma says to me and my mom always questions it.

Chelsi Cunningham

Chelsi is the winner of the children's angel stories. This spirited young lady has many celestial wonders happening in her life. We are all waiting for *HeartBeat Angels II* so we can be enlightened by this heartfelt child.

Angels are Special

One dark and rainy night with a thunderstorm, I was so scared. I was saying my prayers before I went to bed and I lay down, but I was shivering. I got up to look out the window and I fell and scraped my knee on a toy. I started to cry. When my mom came in, I was back in bed and I pretended to be asleep. I looked at my knee and it was scratched up pretty good. I put a Kleenex on it and my knee felt better. I felt a warm touch by someone. My knee did not hurt anymore and I felt safe. There was another boom that shook the whole house so I hid under the covers for a little while. I went to look out the window and it was only raining now and I was happy. I shut my eyes and fell asleep. I know I am safe now when my angel is around me.

Arielle Demers

Age 8

Jordan Turko

Angel Encounter

This is a special angel encounter. I was sitting on my bed when I was five and everyone was sleeping. I was scared but then I felt a strange feeling inside of me. In five minutes I was not scared any more. I went back to bed but it happened again. I was scared again and the strange feeling came back and everything was okay again. I finally went to sleep and I had a dream. The dream told me that the strange feeling I had inside was my angel helping me so I wouldn't be so scared. I don't know why I was scared. That was a special encounter with an angel.

Alyssa Enders

Age 8

I Believe In Angels

I know I have an angel because when I fell on some wood, my leg was not broken. My leg was weak but it was okay. When I played hockey against the moms and dads, I got two goals. When I was in a fight with my sister I didn't even get hurt. When I was on a mountain I never fell off. I didn't even hurt myself when I fell off my bike without a helmet. I didn't even crack my head open. When I was sick and I had to go to the hospital, I got better real soon. I believe in angels because they help me all the time.

Tasha Cerny

Age 8

Madison Blackburn

Really, Really Scared

I have an angel story about the time I was really, really scared. My grandfather was to meet us at the end of the road when my brother and I got off the bus. When we got off the bus he wasn't there, so we walked up the hill but his truck wasn't by the house. We were both really scared because someone was always at home. My brother had a key and unlocked the door and we didn't want to go in. It was so scary. When we did go in, all of a sudden I started to laugh. I laughed and laughed. Everything was so funny and I hugged my brother. My grandfather came in and I was just laughing and laughing. I know it was my angel making me laugh. I will never forget it. It is still funny to me.

Nicholas Hruschak

Age 7

Sara's Angel

When I came home from the school bus, I found out my dad wasn't home so I went to the baby-sitter's. As I started walking to the baby-sitter's place, it started to rain. The rain and all the noise made me very scared. This is what I said to God, "Oh please God, make the rain stop." It was still going for a minute but then it stopped. By the time I got to the baby-sitter's house the rain started again. God and my angel helped me when I was scared and afraid.

Sara White

Age 8

The Fairy I Saw

I was at my Grandma's when I saw a fairy and it was a girl. If I could have seen it longer, I would have drawn it, but I didn't.

If you see fairies, you will be so happy. They bring you luck to your home. So do your best. If you do a favor, you need a fairy there to help you.

I will tell you a story, a real story. I was about seven years old and I was going to the park with my Mom. I saw two fairies following two boys who were crossing the street. One of the boy's fairies had a smile on her face. The other one a present in her hand. I thought it must be his birthday. So I decided to go and say "Hi." to him.

I know I will see those fairies again someday. I thought I could see fairies every day but I was wrong. So I will go on in my life and do what I can in the best way I can. Then I will go to the land of fairies and they will be my children in my next life.

Fawn Auger
Age 9

Rae-Ann Fetting

Scared But Safe

Once I had read a story about strangers before going to bed. I was too scared to sleep, so I shut the window and the blinds, but I was still scared. Next I turned on the light and I read something else. When I got tired, I turned off the light and for some reason I was not so scared anymore. I fell asleep. That night I had a dream. In the dream an angel came and said, "Do not be afraid. God and the angels look after you and love you so you do not have to be afraid". I know I have an angel who helps me with many things and I like to draw and make angels. They make me feel happy.

Rebecca Newman

Age 8

Rayanne Forbes

Randall Kabatoff

CHAPTER 7

Vehicle Experiences

*"The Lord shall be your confidence, firm
and strong and shall keep your foot from
being caught".*
Proverbs 3:26

As we become more con-
scious and aware, we can feel the power of the spiritual
energy. Oftentimes, when we have had an unusual experience occur, we have an awakening in our spiritual life
and as we awaken to a new life, we begin to recognize
that there is something bigger than ourselves. Thus, our
journey begins. As we travel in space or in our vehicles,
we are not always aware of the protectors close at hand,
ready to assist and guide or even take control of situations. Divine intervention is demonstrated in the following stories as they express the attributes of pure love that
we all need.

Randall Kabatoff

Life Review

Life Review describes a psychic phenomenon. I learned about the term during a workshop on para-psychology themes. It is such an unusual life experience; people discard it as a daydream or an illusion of some kind and hesitate to share this experience with others for fear of being considered 'different'. During that workshop, I overcame my fear and shared my story with the group. Here it is.

On a beautiful spring morning, mid-May 1964 in Germany, I was on my way to an important business meeting scheduled for 13:00 hours. The secondary road I drove down had recently been paved and was in excellent condition. In fact, that particular stretch of road headed south in a straight line for seven or eight miles. With hardly any shoulders, the road had deep ditches on both sides. My car was easily speeding at 100 mph. Since there was no speed limit in Germany at that time, I enjoyed giving my car a little workout.

My lane was clear but in the opposite direction an agricultural tractor slowly approached, pulling a load of straw. Suddenly, from behind the tractor-trailer, a car appeared, trying to pass. With seconds to spare, it ducked back behind the tractor as I raced by.

In those few seconds, facing an inevitable head-on collision, I saw my life spread out in front of me. I saw myself as a toddler, a pre-schooler, in class rooms, during bombing raids in Berlin, in service behind the western front, at my high school graduation, on my honeymoon trip, and with my children in the garden of my recently built home. I was able to see all these different events at the same time, both as a toddler and an adult in my mid thirties. It was an overwhelming experience.

On the next turn out, I stopped my car and stepped out for a moment. I found myself drenched in perspiration and out of breath like after a hard run. The pictures of myself in so many life situations had vanished. However, the memory stayed with me. To my surprise, I felt at peace with myself, as if I had passed an important test. I told my wife about the event. It was all so funny, so weird and so unreal. What sense did it make? We decided to keep the story to ourselves.

This experience brought about an essential change in my life, including my attitude towards death. I know this final event of my life will be a difficult and challenging one, yet I can think about it without panic or fear.

Joseph H. Scharfenberger

Randall Kabatoff

How My Angels Saved My Life

It was late at night - not even the change of oncoming headlights relieved the monotony - just mile after mile of smooth interstate highway. I drooped over the wheel in exhaustion. I had to be in Great Falls, Montana by 10:00 a.m. the next morning for a radio interview - with miles to go yet.

I sang and slapped my face to stay awake, carried on mental conversations with my angels and thought about this tour around the western United States. What a joy it had been, bringing lectures and hope to people who had searched endlessly trying to find out who they were and what they were here for. I remembered asking my angels at the start of the tour to help me on the long drives during the tour - especially to help me not hit any animals. I didn't want a string of broken little animals behind me, just because I wanted to tour. And here I was, hundreds of miles from my destination, groggy with sleep.

The next thing I knew, a man's voice was saying urgently, "Sandra, wake up! You're going to hit an animal!"

Without missing a beat, I slammed on the brakes and came to a screeching halt. Sure enough, a frightened bunny stood transfixed in my high beams for a split second before scampering away. Even MORE importantly, I was headed towards a fifty-foot embankment at 100 km. an hour! The car stopped a fraction of an inch from the flimsy guardrail. At that speed, I probably would have been killed.

How clever of my angel to say what he did instead of, "Sandra, wake up! You're going to kill yourself!" I probably would have freaked out and gone right over the edge. Now I realize that our angels use our own wisdom and our desires to help us through the days and nights. That reassurance, that reality, has stayed with me and comforted me over the years.

Sandra Bell

Frank Burman

Road Angels

Are there Angels or Spiritual entities involved in our welfare? I have personally experienced a variety of divine interventions, three of which occurred while travelling on the highway.

The first occasion happened in the early 1970's. I was leaving town alone, on a much anticipated road trip across Canada. I was about ten minutes out, ready to pick up speed on what appeared to be an open road when the phrase, "I smell death on this highway," came into my mind. This same phrase continued for another minute or so until I could not block it out of my head. I decided to slow down. Just as I did, I rounded a corner and saw a three vehicle pile-up occurring right in front of me. Because I had already reduced my speed, I managed to stop and avoid a dangerous collision.

Another time, a few years later, a friend and I took a day trip to Radium, British Columbia in western Canada. After a long day of fun, we were tired and weary but glad to be heading home. My friend was driving so I decided to nap in the passenger seat. Suddenly I found myself being shaken awake in time to open my eyes and see our car heading straight for a mountain ledge! My friend had fallen asleep at the wheel. I managed to miraculously grab the wheel in time and steer us to safety, seconds from crashing.

The third of these road experiences happened on a trip to Calgary, Alberta, Canada in the late fall. The weather worsened as I proceeded on my journey. Rainy drizzle turned to fog. Icy patches appeared on the road as the temperature cooled. By the time I reached Olds, Alberta, about an hour from Calgary, there was no visibility except the glare of taillights ahead of me. While back-to-back traffic raced along the highway on that Friday evening. I felt strongly moved to say a prayer. I desperately asked God to not let me die; my child was still young and needed me. Seconds later, a car roared past and pulled directly in front of me. I hit my brakes to avoid a collision. My car spun on an icy patch, flew into the ditch then sped uncontrollably back into the traffic. 'This is it!' I thought. Then something took over the control of my car. I watched in amazement as the car navigated itself across four lanes of steady weekend traffic and landed in a northbound ditch, unscratched.

This virtually impossible feat instilled in me, even more deeply, a profound belief in Road Angels.

Cheryl Caulder

Randall Kabatoff

Snow Angels

As the meeting drew to a close, I glanced out the window to see blowing snow. I wasn't concerned; my car was in reasonable condition with a full tank of fuel. It had been my dad's car and I had ridden in it through many winters so I was confident it could handle the roads.

The only thought lurking in the back of my mind was that I was not dressed for inclement weather. I had a decent winter jacket all right but I was wearing cut-off jeans. My family and friends have always chided me about my casual approach to winter apparel. To be honest, I've enjoyed the attention that this rebellious streak offered.

The wind and snow picked up in intensity as I approached my turn-off. I could see very clearly the deep ruts and how much difficulty the last vehicle had passing through. Confident in the 'Battleship' to plough through, I swung to the right and pressed down on the accelerator as I began my turn to the left.

I didn't get very far when I realized that the car wasn't going to make it, but I kept the pedal pressed until there was no more forward movement. The car stopped and I slapped my palms against the steering wheel, cursing my own stupidity. I should have taken the main highway!

I tried to rock the car back and forth for a few minutes but it didn't work. I knew that I would have to wait for another vehicle to pass by, or try some digging.

Opening the car door and climbing out, I kneeled and quickly took a few swipes at the drifts with my bare hand. I barely made a dent. Oh, oh, this was not going to be easy. Getting cold, I hopped back inside the car to warm up and prepare myself for the task ahead.

As I warmed my hands, I prayed to God to help me out of the mess I had put myself into. I was more than a little worried. I asked Him to send someone along who could dig me out or who had a cell phone to call for a tow truck.

I felt that I had to give the car one more try. I placed it in reverse and pushed the accelerator. It rocked back a foot so I quickly slammed the lever into first gear and floored it. The car moved forward and didn't stop! It felt like an airplane taking off! Anyone who has been stuck in the snow can tell you the different feel between a car that is towed or is pushed out of a hole versus one that gets out on it's own.

I know that God sent His angels to save me that night. They practically flew me out of that snow bank! I am surprised that all of Creation didn't hear my shout of thanksgiving.

E. Dion Lowe

Randall Kabatoff

A Bag of Mints

Several years ago, my husband, Hank, my brother, Steve and I went on a vacation to Florida, U.S.A. Things were going smoothly as we drove along the freeway. We were having fun, enjoying each other's company and telling stories and jokes.

I had purchased a one pound bag of mints to eat along the way so I opened a small corner of the bag and took out three mints, one for each of us. It was close to lunch time so we were looking for a picnic area. My husband was driving at top speed when I spotted a sign and a cut-off close by. Excitedly, I shouted, "There's one!" Hank hit the brakes and turned with a sudden jerk. He was going too fast for the turn. We flew past the table and onto a field heading for a ravine.

Our hearts were in our throats as we looked anxiously at what lay ahead of us. Suddenly, the car came to a complete stop. Stunned, we stared at the deep gorge below us. We were all in deep silence, not believing the horrific danger, too scared to even move. I felt for the bag of mints, so I could break the silence, but I couldn't find them. "Where are the mints?" I asked, trying to get my brain working again. All three of us began looking for the mints inside the car and under the seats. One pound of mints should be all over if the bag had been broken. My brother remarked that all the windows were closed so they couldn't have gone out the window.

Finally, we had enough courage to get out of the car to view the closeness of the edge. We were about one inch away from going over and down a steep embankment to the gorge below. I kept insisting that we look for the bag of mints. We looked under the car, then inside the car again. Still no mints and no bag. There wasn't a mint to be found, except for the three mints we had in our mouths.

How does one explain such a phenomenon? One can't. However, one can choose to believe in the spiritual world or not. I definitely know that an unseen force saved us from death, while taking the bag of mints as proof. Looking for the mints kept us from panicking and gave us something to think about in place of the danger.

To this day, my brother teases me that I ate the mints, bag and all. Thanks angels!

Anne Marszalek

Randall Kabatoff

Spiritual Communication

I am a visually oriented person and usually need to see something to believe it. I have learned over the last few years, however, that spiritual guidance comes in many forms. Some are visual, true, but I also receive guidance through hearing, feeling, or just knowing. All it takes is a willingness to believe in what we are receiving. This is what my story is about.

A number of years ago, I was driving down a quiet highway with my mother. We made idle conversation as I rounded a sharp curve on the road. For seemingly no reason, at least none my mother could understand, I suddenly slammed on the brakes. As we skidded to a stop, we saw a young child on a bicycle right in front of us! My mother looked at me and asked how I had known to stop. I hadn't known about the child - what I responded to was an overpowering need to stop and stop immediately. I had trusted my 'instincts' and avoided a serious mishap. I had been sent a message and I honored it. Mom just smiled weakly. Though she did not really understand, she was getting used to my 'knowing things'.

We continued on. About twenty minutes later, I commented to Mom that a school bus was roaring up behind me (I am not known to be a slow driver!). Sure enough, the bus pulled into the fast lane and started to pass. When it was about half way past, I again slammed on the brakes. Poor Mom received another seat belt bruise. I had received a flash that the bus was going to cut me off, pulling back into the right lane before it had completed passing me. And it happened exactly that way. Even as I hit the brakes, the bus was already moving into my lane. Its rear bumper missed our car by inches. Mom meekly smiled at me and didn't ask this time. She shook her head and announced that she was going to sleep for the rest of the trip home. We arrived home safely thanks to the wonderful and timely guidance given to me.

Mom made her transition to the Other Side a few years ago. Although she had never really understood how I knew things, she now occasionally contributes to it. She has been in a number of my visions and, most notably, gave my father a real boost prior to some important surgery he had to undergo.

Seriously handicapped, my father could barely hold a pen, let alone write. When it came time to sign the surgical consent form, the doctor handed it to me for a signature. Dad insisted he could sign it so I passed it to him. He authoritatively signed it, much to my amazement, and returned it to the surgeon. As the surgeon walked away, Dad asked for the consent form again. The puzzled surgeon complied. When I asked Dad what was going on, he showed me the form. It was my mother's signature, in her own handwriting! I grinned at Dad and told the surgeon it was okay. Obviously Mom was looking out for him and approved of the surgery. With a big smile on his face, Dad was wheeled off to the operating room.

Margaret Davis

Randall Kabatoff

The Spare Tire

I have many angel stories that I can remember, probably from the age of four or even earlier. This one is more recent and very outstanding because someone witnessed it.

It happened on a long weekend in September, 1995. A friend called from Calgary, asking me to come and drive his car back to Edmonton, Alberta, CA. About fifteen miles out of Red Deer, I had a flat tire. My friend and I changed the tire using his spare. In Red Deer, we stopped at a service station to wash our hands. When I drove the car to the air hose to check the air pressure in the spare, I heard a loud hissing. The tire was losing air fast! I pumped in fifty pounds of air, afraid to add more, hoping to seal the leak. This was holiday Monday. Nothing was open and nobody could help. We checked out many places around the town.

I looked at my friend, "Now what? Do we get a motel or do we take a chance?"

He shrugged, "You're the driver. You decide."

I drove into a parking lot, turned off the vehicle, and prayed for guidance and protection. The answer was revealed that we could continue.

By the time we arrived home, it was around 10:00 p.m. The tire was still up but would surely be flat by morning.

The next morning, the tire was still up. Not believing my eyes, I dug out my pressure gauge. To my horror, it read 80 lb. of air pressure. "No way!" I thought. I would never have put that much air in it. I tried again. Same reading! We drove into Edmonton that day and home again with no problem from the tire. I wanted to get it checked but my friend was tired and wanted to go home. The next morning, we were just at the city limits when I started having trouble handling the vehicle. I drove to a tire shop.

The tire attendant shook his head after examining the tire, "How did you drive it like this?" I told him the full story and he listened in disbelief, "You would not have arrived in one piece if you took this thing on the highway. It would have disintegrated. You could have been killed or even killed someone else!"

I replied, "Would you mind telling the owner!"

Grace Oranchuk

Randall Kabatoff

A Lesson Learned

Although I've always be-
lieved in angels, the Higher Power and intuition, I neither lived on that path of thought nor raised my children
on it. I wanted physical proof of such things. That is the
way I was raised and so were generations of my family
and neighbours before me.

My physical life seemed to drag on, becoming more of an
existence then real living. Then one day, instead of more
anger, annoyance, frustration and joylessness in my life,
something happened, a turning point. Suddenly I heard
myself saying, "Enough of this garbage." Was that the
end of the negative things in my life? Of course not!

I became more ill on all levels of my very being, inside
and out. I needed to part with most of my material pos-
sessions. Grief overwhelmed me, as I moved to another
place. An inner voice of courage kept me going as I tried
to live what society here in North America considers a
normal life. For me, it was not good enough anymore
though I still sat on a huge 'pity pot'. I began a mourning period and realised that God had said we are to be
joyful and happy. So it was up to me and me alone to
change this state of my life.

Suddenly, advertisements for many different types of
enlightenment classes just appeared in my direct vision
and awareness. How could I have missed them so many
times before this? I realized that I hadn't wanted to see
them. I began attending classes and seminars that felt
right for me. Only once did I go to a lecture that my intuition told me was not right for me. It was a lesson learned
that I can share. Go where it feels right for you. Never
mind what friends and relatives say about it. Through all

the courses I took, I very slowly began to really believe in angels and the Great Creator.

But the real heart of this lesson is what happened one day. I do not like driving but I needed to go for supplies even though I was very ill. I began to tremble when I started my vehicle. In desperation, I asked, "Please, someone help me." And I heard a voice say, "I will, if you allow." Since I was alone with the radio off, I had to believe that this voice came from a Higher Power.

This presence now makes himself known to me by a breath of air across my shoulders. One day, about two miles from home, like so many others, I let down my driving awareness. All three lanes of the highway ahead of me had vehicles on them. What I didn't know was that in my exit lane, four or five transport trucks were rolling along very slowly. Of course, I was still travelling the speed limit when suddenly, a great force of wind came through the passenger side of the windshield, passed in front of me and out the driver's side window. It startled me so much; I came back to full awareness and realized that at my speed of travel, I would collide with the trucks ahead of me. I took appropriate action and avoided an accident. Yes, it was my 'driving angel' who warned me.

Since that time, I have learned who that angel is. In fact, I knew this person when he was here on earth. Now I ask him for safety and guidance on every trip I take. I always say, "Thanks," and can feel him smile in acknowledgement.

In conclusion, I wish to say that each one of us has guardian angels. We just need to let go of our 'peopleness' and let the angels into our lives.

Thank you for reading my story. It feels good to tell about this aspect of my life.

Lora Wall

Michael, My Constant Companion

In 1985 I made a decision to study the Bible in depth. To my amazement angelic appearances were documented in the Old as well as the New Testament. At that time I was regularly attending Good Shepard Lutheran Church in Miami, Florida, where the gifts of spirit were recognized, honored and practiced. The congregation was buzzing with like-minded souls, seekers on the spiritual quest of becoming all they can be. I verbalized my desire for angelic encounters only in prayer. The next time I attended the service, before I had a chance to share my request with anybody, a young lady stood up and announced an "angel workshop" she was having in her home and anybody who was interested in attending to contact her. I practically leaped with joy at such a speedy answer to prayer. The workshop consisted of many stories from people who had experienced angelic encounters. We were encouraged to call out for them by name.

I resided in a quaint trailer park, tucked in the midst of government subsidised, low income housing projects; a poverty stricken, drug infested area. Because of this I felt calling on Archangel Michael would be quite appropriate.

I had a neighbor and close friend who worked nights. His daughter, much younger than I , came to visit from Yakima, Washington. Since her dad slept most of the day, Anne and I spent considerable time together. Shortly after her arrival she got very ill. One of her eyes was completely swollen and shut, and she complained of excruciating pain in her kidneys. After checking her temperature, I found she was burning up (104 degrees Fahrenheit).

We got into my car and headed for Jackson Memorial Hospital. The heat was brutal in the middle of the afternoon rush hour on Interstate 95, when I had a blowout flat tire in the middle lane heading southbound. I flipped on my emergency lights and started hand signaling to the right, hoping I would be able to pull off the highway without being squashed. Once safely away from danger, we locked up my little red Hornet station wagon and I lifted my right hand, thumb up and called out loud, "Michael help!"

Within seconds a man in his late 30's pulled over and invited us in. We told him where we were headed and in total silence he drove us to the emergency room. I opened the door and asked,: "What is your name?" "Michael", he said.

All I could say was "Thank you for coming!"

I felt as if I was walking on water. I could hardly contain my excitement. It works! It really works! They do come when we call on them. It was a breathtaking experience, to say the least.

From that day forward when I was driving anywhere at all, before I turned on the ignition, I invited Michael as my traveling companion. I could feel his profound presence and his strength. Several passengers commented that there is "something special" about travelling with me in my car.

Another travelling miracle happened in 1989. I was again taking Interstate 95 from work. As I exited towards my home, there was a traffic light and since it was red, I came to a full stop and waited. When the light turned green, my right foot slid off the gas pedal and shook uncontrollably. I could not fathom what was happening to me, nor did the drivers behind me. They were blowing horns, showing body language of impatience and yelling, but for the life of me I could not stop my leg from shaking. As I looked up, a car came driving through like a flash on my right side with a speed exceeding the speed limit. Had I been in the intersection I would have been demolished. At that instant my leg stopped shaking and I could proceed across the intersection. I was awed, as I am sure were the other drivers, that I witnessed the miracle of Archangel Michael, and profoundly grateful.

Ilonka Baro

Father Douglas, osf
Fransiscan Missionary Brothers

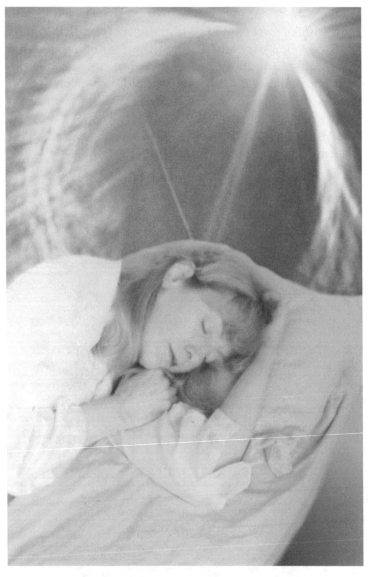

Randall Kabatoff / Sherry Ogg-Kabatoff

Chapter 8

Dream Messages

" We have had dreams but there is no one to
interpret them for us." Joseph said to them,
"Surely interpretations come from God!"
Genesis 40:8

The purpose of this chapter is to help everyone realize the significance of dreams in our everyday lives. Dreams help us find hidden depths of our existence which are out of our reach during waking hours, bringing insight into self-knowledge. Dream interpretations have been recorded on ancient cave walls and stone slabs. The Bible tells us of many different dreams to prophets and saints, including the story of Jesus' arrival. Our dreams create a world where space and time have no limiting power. All time is in the 'now' time frame. Intuitive people seem to regard their dreams as important, and we find that dreams have become part of literature, art and religion, as well as science. Take, for instance, the young boy who dreamed of hovering over the earth and then became a famous astronaut in adult life.

Pauline Lawson

Second Chance at Life

While I was visiting in Guadalajara, Mexico, I had a very disturbing dream. I dreamed that I was killed in a car accident. The dream was so vivid and so real to me, it upset me deeply and I began to cry. I cried and cried without being able to control myself. Finally, I called my sister in Canada and told her my dream. She suggested that I come back to Canada as soon as possible. I took her advice and returned immediately.

My children were visiting in British Columbia, so I asked a friend to drive me there to pick them up. My friend drove while I sat in the passenger seat. As the twelve-hour trip became weary, I dozed off and so did my friend at the wheel. We tumbled down a mountainous cliff. Fortunately, my friend was not too badly hurt. My condition, however, was different.

A helicopter flew me from New Hazelton, British Columbia to the Edmonton, Alberta Misericordia Hospital. I was not aware of my broken body. I had both feet, an ankle and a knee broken along with all my ribs. My left lung was punctured and my lungs began filling with fluid. I heard the doctor say, "We're losing her! Dianne! Dianne! We're losing her! Who do you want us to call?" Slowly I drifted off deeper and deeper. I began talking to God and repeating, "Though I walk through the valley of death," then I asked God to finish the rest of it for me because I was so tired.

My Conversation With God:

God began talking to me and I was taken to a mansion. As I walked through this house, I saw many rooms and asked God what they were for and what all this meant.

God answered, "Haven't you ever heard of Eternity?" I said, "Yes, but I really don't know if I understand it."

"Do you want to go further?" asked God.

I nodded, yes, so we walked on. As we walked past one of the rooms, I saw my father and my brother. They were sitting very still and looking sad. I asked God what they were doing there.

He replied, "They are still learning; they aren't finished yet." We kept on walking farther and God told me that it was all up to me. I could return if I wanted to.

I looked down and saw my body in the intensive care unit. I wondered why I looked so different. I knew it was my body but it seemed so tiny and old. I remembered a young girl, on the heavy side, with bright red, fluffy hair. This person looked much different but it was me.

I asked God how I could get back. He told me to watch the breathing machine. "It is mechanical but when it goes up, you stay in your body, when it comes down, you take a breath too. When you are ready, you can blink your eyes to let your family know that you want to live."

Many years have passed since that dreadful accident but I still remember that wonderful conversation with God. I was in a coma for three and a half weeks. This lesson wasn't over yet because I had to relearn how to talk, to walk and to care for myself. Many scars remain but God gave me a second chance at life. I often get emotional as I tell my story but my connection to God has deepened. Now I appreciate life with gratitude and love. My memory sometimes lapses but my conversation with God stays with me. What can I say but, "Thank you God. I am grateful and I feel special."

YES! THERE IS A GOD!

Dianne Block

Keep on Walking

Angels have visited me many times. They come to protect me and calm my fears. When I am in my darkest hour, they are always there.

On March 21, 1999, I experienced a vivid, disturbing dream. My darling husband of twenty-six years lay dying in a hospital. I sat beside his bed stroking his arm and praying to God for strength. Johnnie lay comatose. Wearing a blue and white gown, he was covered by a yellow quilt. His head rested upon a down-filled pillow. His breathing was shallow and intermittent. In the dream, Johnnie's expression was serene, the pain etched lines erased for the first time in two years. His skin and nails were grey and I was crying because I knew Johnnie was dying. I awoke to hear a clear and gentle voice that said "Do not be afraid, Margie. John must come home."

Seven months from that day, this sad moment became a reality. John suffered a heart attack on October 21, 1999 at 4:30 a.m. He went Home to God's Secret Garden twenty-two hours later. Everything in my dream was sadly true. The coma, the bedding, the colours, the breathing and the serene face all occurred.

The moment my beloved died, a voice said, "Keep on walking. Johnnie is free now."

God prepared me for what has been a grief filled journey.

Margie Shipley

Finding the Church

Our family had meaningful dreams for generations. My mother and grandmother spent a great deal of time interpreting them. I used to tire of hearing about their dreams. 'Such foolish, unrealistic talk,' I'd think. Yet these women were intuitive enough to understand their dreams' importance.

In 1948, when I was ten years old, our family moved from rural western Canada to Oshawa, Ontario, where my father had found a job. We purchased a new brick house with electricity, indoor plumbing and running water - the works. Everyone was delighted. Since we were of the Ukrainian Greek Catholic faith, my mother's next step was to find a nearby church. She asked several neighbors but nobody knew exactly where it was or what street it was on.

My mother became more and more anxious about going to church. Finally, one night she had a dream where she was told how to find the church. My father had to work the next Sunday and my mother did not drive a car so we set out on foot. We left the house around 8:00 a.m. to make sure we had arrived for the 11:00 a.m. service.

My sister and I complained the whole time. We weren't too happy to get up and be ready to leave at such an early hour. Where were we going? Why were we going? What if we get lost? What if we couldn't find our way back again? And so on. Nevertheless, Mother remained positive and determined that she knew the way. We walked and walked but it seemed hopeless that we would ever find the church. We asked people along the way but they weren't certain themselves.

We became afraid that we would be lost forever in this big city. Still, Mother persisted, following her intuition.

Finally, we came to a bridge and she didn't know whether to go over it or under it to the sidewalk along the bottom. A man eventually came along and told us that the church was only four or five blocks away and we could go either way, though the bridge was shorter. By then, my sister and I were absolutely miserable. We had eaten our snack, drank the water and we still had to walk farther. Mother marched on with delight while we trailed along wearily. Finally, we found the church, just in time for the 11:00 a.m. service.

After the service, Mother told everyone who would listen about her dream and her delight in finding the church where she gave thanks to God for his guidance and for our new home. We met a neighbor and her two daughters who showed us a shorter route. Indeed, I would walk this route many years before learning to drive at the age of eighteen. I was later married in the new church that was built across the road.

Dreams truly do have many messages for us, yet we ignore them, forget them and push them away as unimportant. Through the years, I have had many wonderful dreams, which came true. Others were disturbing and unexplainable. It is up to us how we interpret them, for God's messages are not always explainable - just there.

Pauline Newman

Randall Kabatoff

Jesus is Coming

I had a very vivid dream in September, 2000. It was very different from my other dreams because it was in colour. In the dream, I was with my brother-in-law, Allan, in an old fashioned room, when we heard shouts from outside. As we listened, we realised that they were children's voices, perhaps playing. We could hear them shouting, "Jesus is coming, Jesus is coming!"

We went closer to the window to see what was happening. The sky was dull and looked like a big screen. However, we knew it was the sky. Slowly, it began to roll up, starting at the left corner. I can only describe it as a movie screen rolling up from the bottom. The sky became brighter with lots of different colours. Suddenly, we could see Jesus standing in his robe, which was red and blue, not the traditional white. He had bare arms and legs with sandals on his feet. The vision became clearer. A bright light came from behind him. He moved forward and then knelt down to look at something. It appeared that he was picking something up from a basket or box. Each time he would pick it up, look at it and then put it to the side. He did this three or four times. I thought that he was looking for someone's name. 'Is it my turn?' I wondered. Suddenly he faded away and the sky darkened in colour. My brother-in-law and I stood very still. Everything remained quiet while we watched through the window.

Upon awakening, I told my husband my dream. The entire experience had such a strong effect on me. Indeed, it was my turn. In the morning, I felt so relaxed. I prepared for my guests' arrival with such ease, the dream constantly on my mind. Since this dream, I am much more laid-back, relaxed and calm. I feel that I am, indeed, fortunate to have had such a wonderful dream about Jesus.

Pat Turner

Stained glass window designed by Rev. Rinaldo Angelo Zarlenga, O.P., St. Francis Chapel, Arthur Merkle – Clara Knipprath Home, Clifton, Illinois, U.S.A.

CHAPTER 9

Childhood Memories

*"I am the Alpha and the Omega,
the beginning and the end".*
Revelations 21:5

In this interesting chapter, the readers can allow themselves to remember and relive their own childhood secrets of the heart. Suddenly, a certain experience is vividly clear, we remember it exactly as it was in childhood. How exciting to revisit that special moment.

Children find it easy to move to the other side of the veil and experience the spiritual Kingdom. Their world of no boundaries is of limitless creativity that opens the door to communication with the Creator.

As we mature into adulthood, our imagination and our fantasies become distorted by false notions that, if it is imagined, then it isn't real. Definition tells us that imagination is the formation of something not present to the senses, something unreal. Consider, if everything that we see, touch, hear, feel and taste is real, what happens to imagination and knowledge that becomes reality to the dreamer and the inventor.

One of the most powerful experiences an adult can have is to awaken the ability to remember. The heart does not live according to logic and reason. Everything outside of us is a reflection of what is inside of us. Take the time to reflect and renew your childhood spiritual experiences, as the authors have in this chapter.

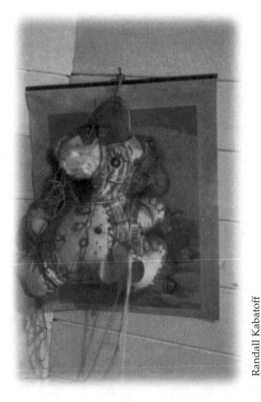

Randall Kabatoff

The Ring and the Green Angel

I know that I have a Guardian Angel. This story is about the time she physically appeared to me. It was in the late 1950's and I had just celebrated my fifth birthday. One of the most precious gifts I received was a birthstone ring from my grandmother. I know now it was not a real emerald but it did not matter. I thought only big girls were given jewelry, so I was quite proud of it.

Shortly thereafter, I became very sick. A trip to a doctor was difficult to arrange. We lived out in the country and the nearest town was a fair distance away. My dad worked away from home most of the time, so transportation for the rest of us was something never taken for granted or easily arranged with neighbors. Telephones were an extravagant luxury we did not possess.

My mother was alone with my two younger sisters - one just a baby - and me. I was running a high fever, so she isolated me from them. I remember her giving me cool baths and changing my bedclothes often because of the fever. When my ring kept slipping off my finger, I reluctantly allowed it to be placed on the highboy dresser beside my bed.

I was lying in my bed and thinking it must be night time because everything seemed so dark. Suddenly, my bedroom door opened and a brilliant light filled the room. In the midst of the light stood a beautiful figure, a lady dressed in an iridescent green fluttering gown. There was so much light around her, I could not make out her features except for her long flowing hair in a color I can not describe. Then she softly spoke and what she said still amazes me. She asked, "Should I take you? Or should I take your ring?"

The next day I was ready for life and breakfast again. I asked my mother who that lady was that visited me and could I now have my ring back. My mother replied that I never had any visitors and that my ring should still be on the dresser. Much to my dismay, the ring was not there. A search of the entire bedroom revealed nothing. I never found my ring.

To this very day I believe in angels and have a special affinity for ones dressed in green!

Katherine

Judy Hamilton

Memory of Thankfulness

I can't recall too much about my childhood. We were the poor family in town and lived on the other side of the tracks. Walking to school one mile, especially in winter, was a real struggle.

One spring afternoon, I was riding my bike home from school when suddenly one of the neighbour boys pushed me off my bike. Needless to say, I landed hard, hitting my head in the process. It knocked me unconscious. As I lay in the middle of the road, my sisters went into shock and began screaming hysterically. They were shouting and arguing about which kid had knocked me down. Meanwhile, I was still lying in the middle of the road.

As I became aware of the screaming and yelling, I remember a voice telling me to get off the road. Dizzily I stood up and staggered over to my bike. I picked it up and moved to the shoulder of the gravelled road. My sisters followed, delighted that I was able to move about again. In all the excitement, no one had noticed an approaching car. All of us barely got off the road before the car whizzed by, spraying gravel everywhere. I never gave this incident any more thought. I didn't discuss it with my parents either. It was just a kid thing.

Life went on, I married, had children and became involved with the family business and the trials which life offers. However, in my fifties, I suddenly began thinking of this dangerous fall. I had a desire to share the experience with my family and friends. This mishap was still so vivid in my memory as I told the story.

Within the last three years I also began to reach out for my spiritual path. The search was on and I was changing. I am getting not only older, but wiser and more in tune with my own mortality. Why wasn't I thankful for my protection from the near accident? I found it strange that I hadn't given this situation more thought. Yet I can still hear the voice saying, "Bernice get up. It is time to get up."

Up until a few years ago I didn't acknowledge God's hand in this experience. I wasn't thankful but I am today. The incident shows that God watches over us even when we don't think about him. This may not seem like a big spiritual experience but it is a thankful one.

Bernice George

Randall Kabatoff

You're Going to be Okay!

$\mathbf{D}$uring the mid 1950's, when I attended grade school in rural Alberta, there were no school buses. My brothers and I walked a mile and a half each way, regardless of the weather. We spent the time trotting along the dirt road, kicking stones, playing in puddles or trying to keep warm in a snowstorm. My two younger brothers walked with me, if we weren't in one of our disagreements. As sibling rivalry goes, I often walked alone.

One day while walking alone, a brief experience changed my life. The memory has remained almost as vivid as the day it happened. The effect on me has carried me through a series of years filled with overwhelming challenges. If I should live to be one hundred years old and enjoy bounties beyond my wildest dreams, that one moment in time on a dusty country road will always be cherished with the greatest affection and highest reverence.

It seems odd that I cannot recall other things surrounding that day. Perhaps the experience has overshadowed all the other details. I don't recall how old I was — about twelve, I think. I don't remember where my brothers were, although they were home by the time I arrived. What I clearly remember is that the day was a most wonderfully warm, summer day. Tall poplar trees bordered the grain fields, birds sang cheerily and the heat from the road's clay soil rose into the air, forming shimmering waves of light. I was on my way home from school and no one was on the road ahead of me, or so I thought.

The road leading to my home was a mile long with a few

hills and a bridge. Across the bridge lay a long, flat stretch bordering the fields for almost half a mile. On the last quarter of a mile before my home, the road rose sharply and leveled off for several yards before connecting with our driveway. From the bridge, however, one could not see past that high hill. As I walked along the flat half-mile stretch, no one was on the road ahead of me. I reached the hill and began working to climb the steep grade. Once I reached the crest of the hill, I was surprised to see a man walking just a few feet ahead of me. How could he be there? I wondered. There was no possible explanation. Admittedly, I was a little frightened.

He didn't look at all familiar. His clothes seemed different too. His pace was so slow that I couldn't stay behind him. I decided to pass him. As I did, he called out, asking why was I in such a hurry. For some reason, I didn't feel frightened anymore. We talked as we walked. I asked him if he would like to visit my parents and me at the house. He gently declined. At the end of the road, we said goodbye. He continued down the road past our driveway. I watched him briefly as he strolled away.

Both my parents were in the kitchen when I arrived. Excitedly, I told them about the man I had just met. I described him but neither of my parents knew him. I thought this very odd since my father was well known for many, many miles around. How could a man walking on foot be from a place so far away that my dad didn't know him? I had to go back and talk with the man again. It had been only a few minutes since we parted. He couldn't be far away.

When I got back to the end of the driveway, the man was gone. I ran down the road to see if he had walked into the fields. He was nowhere in sight. I was sad. How I wanted to be with him again. Slowly I walked back to my house. The last words he said kept running through my mind, "You're going to be okay." They have remained with me ever since. The memory of my Guardian Angel and our meeting, brief as it was, has transcended heartache, loss and fear. I know that I am always going to be okay.

Judy Weir

Randall Kabatoff

A Little Girl's Wish

My father worked for the Canadian Armed Forces, so our family lived in many parts of Canada and other countries. Though often a hectic and sad lifestyle, leaving my friends behind, it gave me a great experience. The downside of moving around every few years was that I didn't visit my extended family often and I knew little of my grandparents.

When I was nine, we were living in Inuvik, North West Territories, Canada. I had not seen any of my grandparents for some time. To my delight, my parents informed me that we were going to visit my grandmother in Moncton, New Brunswick. My grandmother, however, only spoke French so I had to learn a new language in order to speak with her. I eagerly began learning French so I could tell her about school and my adventurous life. I can still remember how excited I was. I kept thinking, "I'm going to visit grandmother!"

One night, I awoke to find a vision of a lady standing at the end of my bed. At the time, I had no idea who she was. She did not speak or even move. She just stood still in a long, grey-white dress which appeared to be transparent. As I watched for more details, I saw that her hair was pulled back in a bun. The lady eventually went away and I went back to sleep.

In the morning, my mother came to wake me and told me that we would not be going to New Brunswick on a holiday. My grandmother had died during the night. Of course, I did not tell my parents about my vision. Instead, I brushed if off as a dream and forgot about it.

The news of grandmother's death left me devastated; I

was so hurt and angry about the trip being cancelled. I remember thinking what a total waste of time it had been to learn French. All that work for nothing. My grand-mother was gone, too. It was a rotten deal and it took some time before I got over it.

As the years went by, I often thought about my vision although I never shared this experience with anyone. Until now, that is. I never had another vision but I do know that it was my grandmother's spirit coming to visit me and say good-bye to a little girl who so desperately wanted to see her.

Now I am a grandmother. Yet, I can still see myself lying flat on my back on a bed in the middle of the room, with end tables on each side. The beautiful lady stood at the foot of the bed.

Thank you for the visit Grand-mere and for letting me know you couldn't wait for my visit. I know we will be together in time, in another space.

Cindy Gabel

Randall Kabatoff

The Old Man

When I was small, maybe nine or ten years old, my family decided to camp in Lodgepole, Alberta, Canada. I was with my siblings, mother, father, and my father's one sister and her children. At this time, I had not learned to speak English; my family spoke in Stoney, which is similar to the Sioux language.

We travelled by horse drawn wagon on this day and a half journey. We made camp in Violet Grove. After that, my cousin Agnes and I began playing a card game with my father. He was the winner and had a game he called, 'whoever loses gets a flick on the forehead with the finger'. I did not like this game, so as he went around the circle doing this, I quickly crawled under a blanket.

I had my face covered when suddenly an old man appeared before me. He was an old native man with long white braids. He was lying down with his hands folded behind his head and he just looked at me. He did not speak or even move. He just stayed in the same flat position looking at me.

I became so frightened that I quickly uncovered my face. My father knew something was wrong since my face was so pale and I looked so afraid. I told my father what had just happened. He never said anything, he just smiled at me.

Later in the evening, more people from our band came to our camp but they kept to themselves. Father later told me that maybe this was the meaning of my vision of the old man. It didn't make much sense to me at the time.

I was always different from the other children when I was growing up and it continued into adulthood. I preferred to explore nature with my grandmother. I went everywhere with her. We picked herbs, berries and other food. She taught me native lore. When I was about fourteen years of age, my grandmother died. Before she passed on, however, she was able to tell me of the future for my people. She predicted everything that is happening now. She prepared me in many ways and with this knowledge I am now able to practice herbal medicine. The Sioux call us the 'Plant People' because we pick herbs. The herbs are used to heal people.

My grandmother was a very special person in my life. I think of her often when I am alone with Mother Nature. I enjoy nature very much. Grandmother taught me to give an offering before I pick anything in nature. I bless them and ask that they help me in finding the correct herbs. Often other blessings will come as well, such as the time a fourteen-point elk came to one of my sons as I gave a blessing.

Dreams are also an important part of my life. I dream of relatives that have passed away, like an uncle or auntie. They tell me what to expect or how to look for solutions for my family and my people.

I think of the old man that frightened me so many years ago and I think that he too, had a message for me. I have never seen another vision but my life has been blessed with so many other things that life has to offer. Perhaps this old man was my guide for this life.

Mary Rain

Our Lady of Light

Our Lady of Light Prayer Card

CHAPTER 10

Miracles From Powerful Prayers

"Only it must be in faith that he asks, with no wavering, no hesitating, no doubting".
James 1:6

Today, testimonials in this field are definitely taking place throughout North America. We don't watch them on TV and they don't make headlines in our newspapers. They are not considered newsworthy. Yet miracles are taking place from powerful prayers throughout our continent and we don't hear about them.

Sister Alice Johnson, author of three books, writes, "Miracles are experienced rather than described. Their heart-transforming dynamism is unique among all human experiences. In particular, apparitions of Mary, Mother of Jesus, have multiplied during the past century with more than 20,000 apparitions in forty countries and five continents".

Many of these 'invisible references' can be found in the Bible, such as in Romans 1:20, "Ever since the creation of the world, his invisible attributes of eternal power and divinity have been able to be understood and have no excuse". It goes on to say that our "senseless minds were darkened".

Indeed, many personal revelations have been published to testify to this. The messages from Jesus and his mother Mary, are requesting that we change our ways. Not only are there messages but miracle healings as well. Visionaries have testified and published books in such places as British Columbia, Ontario, Canada; New York, Ohio and Kentucky, U.S.A., Mexico and Australia to name a few. Many of these amazing occurrences began in 1991 and they continue to the present time.

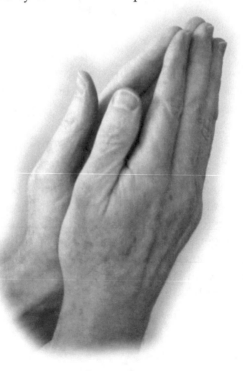

The Witness of Bill White, M.D.

As a medical doctor, I had the privilege of studying neurology and neurosurgery at the Royal University of London, England and Edinburgh, Scotland. This was fifteen years ago. One night, while reading in bed, I experienced a sharp pain in my right shoulder and couldn't move my arm due to muscle spasms. After going to the Emergency Room, I was admitted and treated for Rheumatoid Arthritis. Later, I felt a slight improvement.

Several months later, I was in Edinburgh at Western General Hospital, Department of Neurosurgery. We were repairing the right side of a young woman's skull, which had been destroyed in an accident. It was necessary to stand for a nine-hour operation. It caused me such pain that I was unable to move afterwards. The excruciating pain filled every joint of my body. Now, I had to face the cold fact that my medical career was over.

Since that time I have been 90% disabled, undergoing ten major surgeries in order to retain some function of my arms and legs.

My beloved spouse has had to assist me in all activities of daily living, even simple tasks such as cutting up my food and helping me dress. Watching her pain in knowing that there was nothing else that could be done increased my pain emotionally. All the patented medicines and treatments had little effect and the side effects were toxic.

During the last several years, my hands and feet became almost useless. I was unable to hold a book or even walk to the car. I was at the edge of despair with little hope for the future. It was then that I turned to God and our loving Mother. I offered my pain and suffering for the salvation of souls. I praised God that I could at least use my pain to help others.

I had major surgery in December 1999 to repair massive muscle damage from the arthritis. This was quite painful. It was then that Father Smith suggested that I go with him on a pilgrimage to Lourdes the following spring. I was reluctant to go, but trusting the Lord in faith, I signed up for the trip.

On the pilgrimage through France this past April and May of 2000, I received, through the Batavia Visionary who accompanied us on our journey, three messages from *Our Lady of Light*. These messages are a part of this account because they are not for me alone, but for everyone.

Even though I did not take the baths at Lourdes, I did wash my hands and feet in the water and I have received what I consider a miraculous healing through the intercession of *Our Lady of Light*. My hands and feet are now free of pain for the first time in fifteen years. They are still deformed, however, as a sign to others that the disease was present.

This is the witness that I promised the Blessed Mother I would give in thanksgiving for my healing. Praise God's great Wonder, Love and Mercy.

Sincerely, Bill (Doc) White M.D.,
Cincinnati, Ohio, USA

Messages from *Our Lady of Light* for Bill (Doc) White

April 27, 2000: In a message for Doc White from *Our Lady* at the Basilica of the Sacred Heart, St. Margaret Mary,

Our Lady told the visionary to give me a rose from the ones in front of her statue. Also, to give me this message when I knelt in front of *Our Lady:*

> *"Accept this rose with my love. I thank you for all the roses you have given me. Know that you are a rose in my heart. Know also that through your suffering many souls have been released from purgatory. See how I hold my Son in death. When you suffer, I hold you the same way. I am your Mother and I love you."*

April 29, 2000:

> *"My son - If you are unable to come to me here* (Lourdes), *then I will come to you at home."*

I was in so much pain and so ill that I couldn't walk to the Grotto.

> *"I have heard the prayers of your heart and I accept it. There, I no longer need to offer earthly roses because you have offered the purity of your heart, which continues to blossom into holiness. You please my Son and me very much".*

> *"Know that the healing grace given you was done in order that you may give witness to the glory of God and His wonders. In this way, you will actually help in saving souls by helping them to strengthen their faith. I will accept whatever is your choice...I hold you ever close to my heart and I love you. I am your Mother and thank you for your response".*

I was given the choice of accepting the healing or picking up my cross again for the salvation of more souls. I chose the cross of suffering again, but I did ask that I would be able to kneel at Mass during the Consecration.

May 5, 2000:

> *"My son - I will now give you my words of clarifica-*

*tion in order that you may come to a better under-
standing of the message I gave you during your pilgrimage in a distant land. Know that the offering you
made to take back your cross of suffering in order to
save more souls is sufficient in itself to earn this grace
for others. The purity of your intention pleases the
Father.*

*Just as Jesus carried his cross and then relinquished it
to another, so too have you been relieved of your cross
of suffering. I tell you now that there is no need to pick
it up again. Your healing remains. The testimony of
your healing through the intercession of Our Lady of
Light will save even more souls.*

*Such as Abraham was tested - to slay his son in obedi-
ence to the Father, but then stopped by angels, so too
have you passed a serious testing and your unselfish
action of accepting back your cross has brought joy to
me and to my Son, Jesus. Other crosses await you, but
that one has been removed.*

*I thank you for your obedience to the Father's will. In
regard to your giving testimony to your healing for the
glory of God, it is still my desire that you bear witness
to this grace, and in so doing, you will be helping me
in my mission to convert souls and to lead them to
Jesus. In speaking of your healing to others, I ask that
you distribute my prayer cards (Lady of Light) to them
also. I have promised that graces of healing would flow
through this prayer card. Know that your healing was
part of this promise.*

*My eyes behold you and my heart holds you. My
image (statue) will reflect this to you. I thank you for
your offering and for your love of my son. I told you
that I would come to you at home - and have done so -*

through my image. I wish only to shower you with my love, so be at peace.

Your beloved spouse should remove her doubt and know that she is greatly loved and Jesus smiles on her.

I am your mother and I thank you for your response."

Bill (Doc) White, M.D.

A Brief History

In September of 1991, Mary, the Blessed Mother of God, began appearing as *Our Lady of Light* to a woman from Batavia, Ohio. Later she announced that she would visit her people at St. Joseph Church in Cold Spring, Kentucky at midnight on August 31, 1992. She promised to return, with the Father's permission, in succeeding years on the anniversary of that visit. With her blessing, the site has been changed to Our Lady of the Holy Spirit Center in Norwood, Ohio. On June 3, 1999 she said that August 31, 1999 would mark her last public appearance here.

This prayer card answers a request from Our Lady that prayer cards be distributed throughout America so that all might know she has come here and wishes to be known as *Our Lady of Light*. To honor her request and help to distribute her prayer cards, write to:

**Our Lady of Light Prayer Card
P.O. Box 176236
Covington, KY 41017
Tel 859-331-9393**

The Grotto, Saint and the Angel

Five years ago, while residing in Ottawa, Ontario, Canada, I was hospitalized overnight for an impending lumpectomy. It was the beginning of my long, ruthless battle with fourth stage Non-Hodgkin's lymphoma.

In my hospital bed that night, I felt overwhelmed, lost, and filled with dread. Believing it was possible to block out reality with music, I feebly reached for my Walkman. As fate would have it, my headset clattered to the floor and cracked. This was my breaking point. Choking back sobs of frustration and fear, I thought that my world was falling apart. Suddenly, the tender female voice of my roommate encouragingly said, "Don't cry dear, you can always replace your headset." With swollen eyes, I turned and saw what appeared to be an elderly woman sitting on her bed. Barely managing to speak, I sobbed, "That is not what I'm crying about!" Words and tears spilling out, I confided my worst fears to her. A radiant glow spread over the woman's face. As she spoke, my anguish and fears remarkably subsided.

She introduced herself as a Sister of the Order Montfort. Throughout the next hour, she shared her innermost faith and belief with me. We discussed her favorite Saints and how or why they answered our prayers. She lovingly gave me their pictures. One she noted, was Saint Montfort, who founded her Order and for whom the Montfort hospital we were in was named. She mentioned the Grotto de Lourdes and I became intensely interested when she explained that it was nearby with a statue of Saint Montfort standing there.

I felt little prickles at the back of my neck as I thought back to one particular day after my recent move to Ottawa. While out exploring the city, a sign saying,

'Grotto de Lourdes' intrigued me so I turned and followed the road to its end. Getting out of the car, my eyes scanned a breathtaking view. Here before me was an outdoor chapel with stone walls and a stone altar that housed a statue of the Blessed Virgin Mary. Plaques of gratitude stood everywhere from families for whom miracles were granted. Looking upward, a snow-white replica of the crucifixion stood atop a hill. It left one believing that Jesus indeed looked down upon the many who came to pray for miracles. And here, miracles were granted. I also recalled a statue of a male saint whose name meant nothing then. Now I knew it was Saint Montfort, the saint this elderly lady spoke of.

After this brief reflection, I turned my attention back to her. With a wide smile visible in the bright light around her, she spoke her final words, "Miracles do happen."

My family visited the Grotto. There, they prayed for my life and a miracle occurred. I am still alive.

I shall never forget my Angel who was there for me during my darkest night.

Dale Pearson

A Grateful Nurse

My name is Peggy Hock and I am the school nurse at McAuley High School in Cincinnati, Ohio, U.S.A. On August 3, 2000, I was completing my morning run when I was clipped from behind by a large, unconfined dog and fell to the ground. I took the full impact on my head, suffered a fractured skull and three large inter-cranial bleeds. I underwent cranial surgery at the University Hospital and lay comatose in the Neuro-surgical Intensive Care Unit.

Many prayers were being said for me. Mrs. Cheryl Sucher, the principal of McAuley High School, organized a healing mass. She had suffered from a serious liver ailment a year earlier and had given many testimonials to *Our Lady of Light*. Faculty and administrators helped organize the outdoor mass for me at the school. The pastor of St. Ignatius Church, Mrs. Sucher's parish, led the service. Many family, friends, and colleagues were in attendance. *Our Lady of Light* prayer cards were distributed at the liturgy.

When I awoke from the coma and spoke, their prayers continued, especially to *Our Lady of Light*. In three weeks I was walking, talking and improving. My neurosurgeon said it was a miracle. He had never seen anyone with the extent of my head injuries walk three weeks after the injury. In fact, he said most were still comatose. I have now returned to work as the school nurse at McAuley High School.

I learned many things as I recovered from this critical injury. The most important lesson was a much clearer understanding of the healing power of prayer, kindness, and love. I am most grateful to all who offered prayers for me and to *Our Lady of Light*.

Peggy Hock

Little Voice

My family is close because we had to be. We depended on each other because, in all honesty, there was no one else to turn to, no one who gave a damn.

We were poor and mom waited on tables at the local diner. No, not us, we weren't poor. We were three kids and a mom living on welfare in a small hick town. You knew us. I know you did. Everyone did. We were that one family who stuck out, that one family who was the butt of every joke, whose path was trailed by constant snickers, whose kids were chased home every day under a hail of rocks and whose mom cleared a wide berth at the grocery store on double coupon day. That was us: Reg, Jen, Mom and me - the close family.

I wish it was because of something we did, some small, stupid transgression, anything to justify all that hatred poured in buckets onto us. But it wasn't us. No matter how much I wanted it to be otherwise, we had no hand in it. You could see it on the first day as they came out of their houses to stare at our old pickup clanking past. Their eyes were pasted on its every crack and rusted dent, unforgiving of its potential weakness, ready to use it for quick reference later. Their mouths drooled open, incapable of containing their spite-filled spit at least until we rumbled out of view.

Mom told us not to worry, that they were only curious because we were new and that she loved us. "We'll be okay," she said, "because we're together."

Then Richard, with one happy smirk on his face, told us to "Shut up, all of you! Just sit there and don't even breathe or I'll run all you retards into the ditch!" Good old Richard. He was the cherry on the sundae in the hell that was our lives for the next six months.

Yep, it isn't too difficult to catch my meaning is it? Reg, my little brother, got the worst of it. He was skinny and gawky, at that age when one is all arms and legs and feels like they'll never fit into normal. He was Richard's little rag doll, thrown around like there wasn't even a person inside the button-mouthed exterior. And Jen, my sister, I don't even want to guess. She doesn't talk about it much and I don't really ask. Some of those memories are better left to die in the dirt where they belong.

We had gone through a brutal week with Richard raging all the time and the four of us desperately obeying his every word, careful of every cough, watching every twitch, praying he wouldn't come after us with his frothing fists. We were lucky this time. Richard decided to go hunting for the weekend, giving us a few precious days where we could snatch a little happiness when he wasn't looking.

We prayed as usual that night, kneeling beside mom's bed. "We're so unhappy. Jesus," mom said softly. "Please help us. Please help us find a safe place to be together and to be happy. Get us away from Richard, please Jesus. We don't want to be hurt again." We prayed like this every night, crying and clutching hands, our own little white-knuckled chain of sadness.

Reg and I went to our room across the hall while Jen stayed with mom. Reg and I drifted off for what seemed only two minutes when a light so bright, right through your eyelids bright, shot us straight out of sleep. It was as if my eyes had been open to see it but they weren't. I'll never forget it. We ran into mom's room the second after, yelling and screaming. "What was that? Mom! Mom! What was it?"

Mom and Jen were crying quietly, cradling each other and mom said, "It will be all right. We'll be taken care of."

"What do you mean?" we asked her. "What was it Mom?"

"It was an angel, an angel came and it's going to be all right. Jesus will take care of us. Now come here, both of you. We'll sleep together tonight." So we all wrapped up tight, crying a little, laughing a little and thanking Jesus until we fell asleep, for once, with smiles warming our lips.

We woke to loud, repeated banging. "Linda! Linda! Come on, it's Barb, honey. Open the door!" We raced downstairs, surprised to see Barb, Richard's sister, who really didn't visit much. She raced in, a flurry of determination.

"I'm getting you guys out of here. Kids, help your mom pack. There's a house ready and waiting for you but let's try to hurry, okay?"

We were gone in two hours: away from the town, away from Richard, away from it all. What we had seen that night changed us and fortified us. Now we have this wealth of faith that we always had before but were just unable to dive into or, were maybe too afraid to put on our full faith and see what lay under the surface.

I don't think mom will ever be able to fully describe what she saw face to face in her room that night. And you know what? I couldn't care less because the Lord has shown his hand too many times in my life since then to need any reassurance or proof. I don't need to see it all to believe. I just believe.

Brenda LePage

Chapel Angel

After my husband Carl's colon cancer surgery, he began to experience a blockage in the bowel. The prognosis was not very good. At the hospital, we tearfully spoke of our love to one another. When the nurses came to take him to the operating room, we said our good-byes, not knowing if we would see each other again.

I went to the hospital chapel. There I found a woman very upset. Her husband was very ill in the heart ward. We introduced ourselves and began talking. Tears welled up as we took turns talking about dealing with the pain of our situations. I asked if she would like to pray. We prayed together as we clung to each other. Through the tears and prayers, I felt a certain peacefulness come over me. I do not know how long we were in the chapel but as we were leaving she turned and said to me, "Your husband will be okay but I see a cloud over mine."

Carl made it through the surgery. The next day, when he was resting comfortably, I went to tell the good news to the lady from the chapel. I went to the hospital wing she had told me her husband was on but it was closed. At the nurse's station, I asked if the woman's husband was moved to another wing. The nurses said that there never had been a person by that name in the hospital.

The question is - was this lady an angel sent to me in my hour of need? I believe she was.

As told to Florence Trautman.

Hospital Angel

My husband was in the Canadian Air Force and we were stationed in Germany. During this time a polio epidemic broke out. I was taken ill and it wasn't known at first if I was one of the misfortunate ones or not. As I became increasingly worse, having difficulty swallowing, I was sent first to the Canadian Forces Hospital and then transferred to the American Military Air Force hospital in Heidelburg, Germany. There I underwent many tests including a spinal test, which revealed that I did indeed have polio. It was located in my throat - one of the worst types - Boulber polio.

At this point I was extremely ill, barely surviving. I couldn't eat or drink; swallowing was too difficult. Doctors told me that if I passed the critical 13-day stage, I would survive and be all right. I was very determined to beat this illness since I had a wonderful husband and two beautiful children at home waiting for me. This became my focus. I began to pray, harder and more sincerely than I ever had in my life.

By the eighth day I was critically ill. It was supper time and my tray lay beside me. The smell of the food nauseated me and I wanted it taken away. I began ringing for the nursing sister. I prayed and rang for a long time. No one came. The smell was so strong and upsetting, yet I was too weak to get up and move the tray.

Suddenly, a black male nurse dressed in a white shirt and black pants came into my room and asked what I wanted. I asked him to take the tray away because the smell made me sick. As he removed the tray, he began talking to me in a soft, gentle voice. He told me not to worry and that everything would be all right. He said, "You will be fine," and left the room with my tray. Instantly, a surge of peace came through me. I felt bewildered by its suddenness.

When the nursing sister arrived, she asked, "Where's your food tray?"

I explained to her how I rang and rang for her. I asked her why she had sent the black male nurse instead of coming herself. Her reply stunned me.

"Oh, my dear, you must have been dreaming. We don't have a black male nurse on this ward or even in the hospital for that matter." She consoled me, patting my hand and saying, "There, there, my dear, you were dreaming!" Laughingly she left the room.

I knew that I was not dreaming. My tray was gone from the room. I didn't bother to explain or argue with her. The next day, I suddenly felt better and was soon able to go home.

I did conquer the disease and I thank God for my speedy recovery and for sending me an angel in my hour of distress. Now, over thirty years later, I can still envision the black male nurse standing by my bed, comforting me, giving me hope and incredible strength to deal with life's trials and sorrows.

Anne Marszalek

A Miracle Took Place

I am in my thirteenth year as principal of McAuley in Cincinnati, Ohio, U.S.A. and I want to share my story about the power of prayer.

While in the Good Samaritan hospital from November 8 to 11, 1999, I was given an *"Our Lady of Light"* prayer card. Simultaneously, I was told that if my highly inflamed liver did not stabilize within forty-eight hours, I would be placed on the emergency liver transplant list at the University of Cincinnati Medical Centre. With the prayer card placed on my liver, I stabilized in twenty-four hours.

On December 7, 1999, I had a liver biopsy. My blood would not coagulate. My blood pressure went from 150 to 104 in fifteen minutes. I prayed to *Our Lady of Light* then put the prayer card on my incision. My blood immediately coagulated and my blood pressure went to 118, a normal reading, and stayed there.

On January 4, 2000, I was told that along with my chronic auto-immune hepatitis, I had a dangerously high white blood count. I was severely anaemic with a hyperactive thyroid. My doctor suspected I also had an auto-immune blood disease or auto-immune bone marrow disease. Neither were the results of the inflamed liver. Dr. Weber suspected my entire immune system was collapsing.

I never stopped praying from January 4th until the doctor's appointment on January 11th. On January 9th, a healing mass was said for me at our parish, St, Ignatius. I was told all of McAuley High School was there, along with many friends. On January 10th, I went for my blood tests and prayed as they drew the tubes of blood. At the

doctor's office on Tuesday, January 11th, A MIRACLE
TOOK PLACE!

• My anaemia was much improved

• My white blood count was normal

• There was no sign of a hyperactive thyroid

Thank you for your prayers. They worked! I know God
will help me keep this auto-immune Hepatitis under control.

Cheryl Sucher

From Our Lady

"In days past, God sent His
rainbow to His people as a
sign of hope after He flooded
the earth. In these days God
has sent me, your heavenly
mother, as a sign of hope for
your land of America. So, you
see, the rainbow is significant
in my appearances here as
'Our Lady of Light.'...There-
fore it is my desire that the
prayer card...carry this sign of
hope (the circular rainbow)
which is my signature...Know
that through these prayer cards
many miracles and graces will
flow from the Father. This is
His gift to me and my gift to
all of my children."

—To the Batavia Visionary
1/31/96 and 2/11/96

Lady of Light

Oh, Lady of Light,
Shining so bright,
Be with us this day,
Guiding our way.
Oh, Lady, Oh, Lady of Light.

Oh, beautiful Lady,
Glowing so bright,
Your eyes softly beaming
And gleaming with light.
Oh, Lady, Oh, Lady of Light.

Oh, wonderful Mother,
I feel you so near.
Your presence dissolves
All of my fears.
Oh, Lady, Oh, Lady of Light.

Your comforting arms
Reach out to all.
Your gentle voice whispers
A low pleading call.
Oh, Lady, Oh, Lady of Light.

You wait there so patient
And keep us in sight.
Thank you, dear Mother,
Our Lady of Light.
Oh, Lady, Oh, Lady of Light.

Our Lady of Light Prayer Card

Afterword

"Ask and it will be given to you; seek and you will find;
knock and the door will be opened to you."
Matthew 7:7

After compiling *HeartBeat Angels*, I have learned more about myself, the bond I have with others, and the universe. My connection with God has also increased. There is a fundamental source of knowledge and comfort in knowing that there is someone 'else' looking after me. I do not have to worry about what is going to happen tomorrow because I leave it to my angelic guides to show me the way.

As I read my own stories, I realized that so much was kept a secret for so long. At first I shared my experience, only to have my friends and relatives tell me that I was wrong. In my heart, I knew that I had a spiritual experience, and this made me feel special. However, I kept my secret locked up until now.

For every story that is included in this book, there are countless others just as inspiring. Without exception, every author appreciated having the opportunity to put their story into words in order to share with their loved ones. Many writers have thanked me for giving them space in this creative book – *HeartBeat Angels*.

The value in writing personal celestial experiences is a healing process. Now each of us can move on with this newly acquired inspiration. What a unique challenge we encountered.

I hope that you found these stories enjoyable and as moving as I have found them to be. If some of you would like the opportunity to write your own stories, the following pages are reserved for you. Your story can become a family keepsake.

I encourage you to write your spiritual experience, regardless of its significance. This releases other hidden thoughts that you can share with your loved ones.

I invite those that are ready to share their spiritual encounters, big or small, brief or lengthy, to contact me for the next book which is now in progress.

"Blessed Be God Forever"...

Pauline Newman

Father Douglas

My Story

My Story

About the Authors

Sandra Bell is a former radio broadcaster, currently a professional writer, professor with America Leadership College. She resides with her Kiwi husband in Calgary, Alberta.

Tracee Biletski is a wife, and mom of 3. She worked for the Alberta Government for 8 years, now has a home based business, and is a member of the Spruce Grove, Alberta, Chamber of Commerce.

Cheryl Caulder is a certified practitioner with 25 years of experience in the field of education, social work and alternative healing.

Margaret Davis lives in Ottawa, On., CA. She is a retired army officer and teaches meditation for the soul. E-mail: meditate@magma.ca.

Eagle Woman (Rita Makkannaw) resides west of Edmonton, AB. CA. She continues to learn from the aboriginal Traditional Elders and helps others on their spiritual path. E-mail: ritama@telusplanet.net

Dr. Lila Fahlman lives in Edmonton, AB. CA. She is founder of Canadian and World Council of Muslim Women and University of Alberta Chaplain for Muslims.

Peggy Hock is a school nurse and she resides in Cincinnati, Ohio, U.S.A.

Delores Jack is an educator with a special interest in angels. She resides in Edmonton, AB. CA. E-mail: djack @compusmart.ab.ca

Sherri Jacklin lives in Saskatoon, Sask., CA.; she is a wife, mother, and enjoys writing and crafts. Her story, "The Rabbit" won the second prize.

Randall Kabatoff, B.A., who has a social worker and social psychology background, is dedicated to social change through multicultural and cross spiritual bridge building. He is a writer, photographer and publisher. E-mail: randall@visionimages.ca   www.visionimages.ca

Ann Keane is a nurse, leader, mother of 2. She is a soul being with passion and compassion. Ann lives her life in congruence with her Highest Mission doing the very best. She is author of *Soul Work* and *Mission Driven*.

Yvonne Law resides in Edmonton, AB. CA., along with her partner Jeffrey and their 2 poodles. Yvonne is pleased to share her personal spiritual story with readers.

Janet MacLellan, along with her husband Phillip, owns St. Joseph and the Angels Emporium in Edmonton, AB. CA. The bookstore has the largest selection of rare and out of print Catholic Books in Canada. E-mail: stjosang@telusplanet.net

Linda Malekoff lives in Edmonton, AB. CA., and is a social worker who also enjoys reading and writing.

B.J. Marcou is a terminal cancer survivor and personal health counsellor, wife, mother and grandmother.

Grace Oranchuk lives in rural Stony Plain, AB. CA. She has been on a spiritual journey since age of five. Her belief is *"Ask and you shall receive"*.

Jacki Owens lives in Calgary, AB. CA., is a wife, mother and grandmother, and recently has taken up writing and is looking for more publications. E-mail: aowens@home.com

Mary Rain lives in Duffield, AB. CA. and is an elder at the Paul Band Reserve. She is a native herbalist and a healer that is truly connected to Mother Earth.

Joe Scharfenberger is a business college graduate from Hamburg, Germany, a retired registered nurse who worked in psychiatric counselling for many years.

Cheryl Sucker, wife, mother of 4 children, lives in Ohio, Cincinnati, U.S.A. She has been a principal for 13 years and is very active in the Catholic Church activities.

Esther Supernault is an editor and writer, living in the Stony Plain, AB. CA. area. She is currently in the process of publishing her fifth book, *"When We Still Laughed,"* a Canadian historical novel about a young Cree warrior who is as stubborn as his companion, a young Irishman call Mac. Esther is a nurse with a bachelor's degree in psychology. A mother of two and the grandmother of two. E-mail: cesuper@telusplanet.net

Florence Trautman farms with her husband Clarence in the Stony Plain, AB., CA. area. She started writing un-expectedly about 10 years ago and has published in Canada and the Unted States.

Dr. Bill White, M.D., is a retired neurosurgeon, who resides in Cincinnati, Ohio, U.S.A., and he is an arthritis survivor.

Ruth Yanor-McRae is a master herbalist and iridologist. She practises in Edmonton, AB. CA. along with the native culture. E-mail: rym@telusplanet.net

About the Artists

Frank Burman is a visual artist, based in Edmonton, whose work ranges from fineart painting to commercial illustration in a variety of styles and media. Contact him at: artists@visionimages.ca or www.visionimages.ca

Father Douglas is an ordained Decon and member of the Fransican Missionary Brothers in Edmonton, Alberta, Canada. He is a professional artist who also enjoys stain glass work.

Michael Godet, a Canadian born artist, specialising in imaginative murals, and spirit-infused portraiture. E-mail: mrgaudet_art@hotmail.com

Judy Hamilton, a professional artist from Edmonton, Alberta, Canada. She has her B.F.A. from the University of Alberta. E-mail: jajhamilton@ home.com

Vance Hilton is a professional visual artist based in Edmonton, Alberta, CA. www.vancehilton.50megs.com E-mail: vancehilton@hotmail.com.

Randall Kabatoff, B.A. is a visionary artist/photographer who blends images to portray our spiritual and multi-leveled reality. E-mail: randall@visionimages.ca. 780-414-0866 www.visionimages.ca Edmonton.

Pauline Lawson began her studies in 1955 in England. She is now living in Gibsons, British Columbia, Canada. In 1990 she began to paint angels and icons.

Diane Mitchell has been an artist for 20 years. Her specialty is florals. She is the administrator of the Little Church Gallery run by Allied Arts Council in Spruce Grove, Alberta, Canada.

Maureen Stefaniuk is a visual artist who draws on her Ukrainian/Byzantine spiritual roots, contemporary creation/ feminist spiritualities as well as her own experiences as a single mother of a chronically ill, physically disabled daughter.

Judy Hamilton